SHORT CUTS

INTRODUCTIONS TO FILM STUDIES

CRIME FILMS

INVESTIGATING THE SCENE

KIRSTEN MOANA THOMPSON

WALLFLOWER

LONDON and NEW YORK

A Wallflower Paperback

First published in Great Britain in 2007 by
Wallflower Press
6 Market Place, London W1W 8AF
www.wallflowerpress.co.uk

A catalogue record for this book is available from the British Library

ISBN 978 1 905674 13 8

Book design by Rob Bowden Design

Printed in Great Britain by Antony Rowe Ltd, Chippenham, Wiltshire

CONTENTS

list of illustrations

acknowledgement

LIST OF ILLUSTRATIONS

ACKNOWLEDGEMENT

I would like to thank Paula Massood for reading this manuscript and my other work. She has been an invaluable friend and editor.

INTRODUCTION

From the tabloid press to pulp fiction, and from the stalwart television franchises *Law and Order* and *CSI: Crime Scene Investigation* to movies about serial killers, gangsters and private eyes, film, television and popular culture reflect our continuing fascination with crime. From French tales of professional assassins (*Le Samourai* (1967), *La Femme Nikita* (1990)) to notorious murders in New Zealand (*Beyond a Reasonable Doubt* (1980), *Heavenly Creatures* (1994)) or violence in the slums of Rio De Janeiro (*City of God* (2002)), every national cinema has created crime films. Many cultures have celebrated and mythologised the figure of the bandit, from India (*Bandit Queen* (1994)) to the United States (*The Adventures of Robin Hood* (1938)) and Australia (*The Story of the Kelly Gang* (1906)), and some national cinemas have developed culturally specific crime genres, like the Japanese yakuza film or American gangster film. However for reasons of space, this study will necessarily restrict its scope to British and American films.

Definition, spectatorial pleasures and social meanings

First, what do we mean by crime? Although we often refer to immoral or socially inappropriate acts as crimes, a crime is a very specific legal term that refers to conduct which has been proscribed or forbidden by legislative act (Congress or Parliament), and which is different from actions that are forbidden in civil law (such as not to slander people or break contracts). In the law, crime is defined in two ways, as either *mala in se*, that is acts which are defined as intrinsically bad or 'crimes against the laws of nature' (such as murder), or secondly as *mala prohibita*, that is offences 'against the laws of society' (such as prostitution). Consequently, defining a specific action as a crime is always a social and political act (Friedman 1993: 3–4). Second, the law requires that a crime must have two components, both of which must be proven: that the defendant had the requisite *mens rea* (state of mind) and *actus reus* (voluntary act or act of omission). From punishment to deterrence, the law has multiple functions, and shapes public behaviour by prosecuting those who break laws. Consequently the history of the law and the criminal justice system is a history of dominant power structures and cultural norms, and also tells us something about the history of disciplines like psychology (what is mental illness?), sociology (who are social deviants?) and criminology (what is crime and how is it punished?).

How do we begin to define what a crime film is? Can crime films be defined by their narrative content, or are other elements like style of definitive importance? Can they be defined in terms of their effect on the viewer? If their effect is one of suspense, how does this overlap with the thriller, which also relies upon suspense? Martin Rubin notes that many of the key attributes of the thriller – the transformation of the ordinary, the presence of the exotic, the figure of the labyrinth and the construction of suspense – can also be found in different types of crime films; the thriller is made up of many different genres and sub-genres, and a number of these are also types of crime film, such as the detective and murder stories (1999: 35ff). The crime film is an example of what Nicole Rafter usefully describes as a conceptual 'category', or umbrella term, which encompasses many genres, sub-genres and film cycles, including the cop film, police procedural, action film, courtroom drama, gangster genre, woman's thriller, film noir and so on (Rafter 2006: 3). (She goes on to suggest that there are eight major types of crime stories: the mystery detective story, the thriller, the caper, the tale of justice violated/restored, the disguised western, tales of revenge and vigilantism, the criminal biopic and the episodic action story.) Some of these crime stories have been included within industrial categories, such as the gangster film, while others such as noir and neo-noir have been historical terms created by film critics. Others, like the erotic thriller, which is discussed in chapter three, have appeared relatively recently. A preliminary working definition might be that a crime film foregrounds the commission of a crime, and/or emphasises its investigation, prosecution, prevention and/or punishment. Second, although the commission of crimes can be found in many other genres, including the western, action, science fiction and war genres, violence is a 'signature gesture' of the crime film (Browne 2000: 14). But it is not just the representation of any form of violence but rather the illicit violence of the criminal and the socially-sanctioned violence of the forces of law enforcement that are foregrounded in crime films. The writings of French theorist and critic René Girard on violence are useful here (1979; 1986). Girard argues that the criminal acts as a sacrificial scapegoat whose violent acts symbolically enact the desires and rivalries of the community, but whose execution fulfills society's need for ritual bloodletting and punishment. The fall of the gangster in classic films like *Little Caesar* (1930) and *The Public Enemy* (1931) represents the ritualised disposal of a figure whose violent entrepreneurial actions are merely an extreme and transgressive form of capitalism. Christopher Sharrett has argued that French critic Georges Bataille's theories offer a different understanding of violence than the Girardian model. Bataille understands traditional sacrifice as a transgressive release of excess irrationality, and one that offers a challenge to societies otherwise organised around consumption. For Sharrett, both Bataille and Girard see 'sacrificial violence permeating human interchange and functioning as a basic metaphor for experience (1999: 427). But unlike Girard, Bataille's notion of sacrifice is not rooted in the scapegoat; rather, for Sharrett, Bataille's sacrifice is 'an immersion in the destructive element: a site of transgression' and nihilism (ibid.). This nihilstic violence might bring to mind the sheer destructive pleasure of the gangster Cody Jarrett (James Cagney) shouting 'Made it ma! Top of the world!' as the gas tank he stands on explodes at the end of *White Heat* (1949).

Up until 1970 many crime films foregrounded some social problem – such as prison brutality, police corruption or urban crime – but also offered the solace of that problem's resolution. For example, American gangster films of the 1930s showed the rise of celebrity criminals like Al Capone in fictionalised form in films like *Scarface* (1932), but also showed their punishment and/or death. By contrast, later British gangster films like *Noose* (1948) or *The Long Good Friday* (1981) usually focused on the decline of the gangster's empire, rather than following a rise-and-fall narrative. After 1970 a more critical tradition emerges, which refuses the moral simplicity of earlier crime films and that was often alienated or cynical in its tone (Rafter 2006: 14–17). For example, *Body Heat* (1981), which is examined in chapter three, shows a femme fatale seducing a man to commit murder, which leads to his imprisonment and her successful escape to enjoy the profits of her crime. *A Clockwork Orange* (1971) shows a sadistic juvenile delinquent's pleasure in killing, while *Henry: Portrait of a Serial Killer* (1986) is about a serial killer methodically carrying out his crimes without any ultimate punishment or retribution.

How is the law and crime represented in fiction and film? Who are the figures of authority in crime stories – the detective? policeman? private eye? psychologist? – or criminal? Film and television play a key role in representing and shaping public perceptions about the nature and frequency of crime, as well as the efficacy or otherwise of the criminal justice system. Second, crime films also raise issues about the relationship between the public sphere and the actions (and privacy) of the individual, and at different historical moments have shaped attitudes to different social practices, including sex and drugs. Third, crime films mythologise, and can turn criminals into celebrities or folk heroes like Bonnie and Clyde or villains like Ted Bundy. As the trials of everyone from Rosco 'Fatty' Arbuckle to Bundy and O. J. Simpson have demonstrated, along with the more recent acquittals of Robert Blake (for murder) and Michael Jackson (for paedophilia), trials are compelling spectacles. For example, the sensational murder of Bobby Franks in 1924 by Leopold and Loeb combined a sociopathic thrill-killing with the frisson of a homosexual relationship, and would be the subject of a 1929 play and at least three movies, including *Rope* (1948), *Compulsion* (1959) and *Swoon* (1992). In other words, whatever our personal experience of crime may be (which may vary enormously based on factors of nationality, class, gender and race), we also all experience violence and crime as *representation* mediated through words and pictures: on television, in the newspaper, in pulp fiction, on the internet, in video games and in the movies.

Why then do we watch crime films, and why do they continue to be enormously popular? Like all cinema, crime films offer escapism and voyeurism, or in other words the pleasure of watching stories about illicit worlds and transgressive individuals, from the criminal mastermind in *Dr Mabuse der Spieler* (*Dr Mabuse the Gambler*, 1922) to the serial killers in *The Silence of the Lambs* (1991). We may watch crime films because they offer characters and stories that dramatise transgressive behaviours that may appeal to our fantasies and desires. Perhaps we watch some crime stories because, as with horror films we enjoy being scared, or as Isabel Pinedo describes it, we enjoy 'recreational terror', a spatially and temporally limited experience of fear, akin to a rollercoaster ride (1997: 41). We also may enjoy watching professionals and learning about the unusual yet fascinating details of their jobs. Through police officers, criminalists, psychological profilers and private eyes, we also get a glimpse into criminal psychology, behaviour and cultural practices. Mystery and heist stories offer us intellectual puzzles which chapter one will explore in further detail. Some crime films may offer us *schadenfreude* or a pleasure in others' misfortunes, for we may be fascinated by the villain but also wish to see their downfall. As a character observes in Stanley Kubrick's *The Killing* (1956): 'You know I have always thought that gangsters and artists are the same way in the eyes of the masses. They are admired and hero-worshipped but there is always present an underlying wish to see them destroyed at the peak of their glory.'

Elayne Rapping suggests that the crime story 'sketches out the human (or subhuman) contours by which we distinguish "deviance" from "normality", and the "outlaw" from the "good citizen"' (2003: 50). The relationship between crime literature and/or film and real-life crime has long been a close one. Since the Enlightenment, Western culture began to see human nature as fundamentally rational and good, shifting away from the theological worldview that humans are sinful. With the Renaissance's shift to secular humanism in the late sixteenth and early seventeenth centuries, murder replaced heresy and treason as the ultimate social transgression. Crime began to be understood as an isolated moment of 'uncontrolled passion' that temporarily separated the criminal from the law-abiding citizen. With the rise of the adversarial system in Anglo-American jurisprudence, the trial lawyer replaced the clergy's religious assumptions of sin and evil with secular ideas about motive and behaviour. In her study of American crime fiction Karen Halttunen suggests that producing and reading crime stories are a form of *cultural work* in which society comes to terms with this deviance or social transgression. By the nineteenth century, popular responses to murder were characterised by two recurring elements: *horror* – or inflated language and graphic treatment which prompts a mixture of fear and disgust from the reader; and *mystery* – in which the incomplete, fragmented narratives of a crime preserve a fundamental incomprehensibility which the reader will never completely grasp. These two aspects – horror and mystery – are also central elements of crime films (1998: 1–6). Finally, crime stories have a close relationship to pornography in that both may fuse narrative sex and violence, and like gangster and serial killer films offer graphic and violent spectacle as a compelling attraction for the viewer.

Crime films also point to changing social beliefs about the causes of crime, and at different times have emphasised biological, environmental, aspirational or psychopathological explanations (Rafter 2006: 64–72). Gangster films of the 1930s emphasised both the environmental causes of urban crime and the economic aspirations of criminals, whereas the very titles of films like *Born to Kill* (1947) and *The Bad Seed* (1956) imply crime has biological roots. Where these latter films suggest a deterministic view of crime, aspirational crime films understand crime as an act of free will, motivated by an ambitious desire to rise or escape from poverty or class, as with *The Asphalt Jungle* (1950) and *A Place in the Sun* (1951). Crime films which turn to psychological explanations may be based upon Freudian interpretations, as with *Psycho* (1960) or *Dressed To Kill* (1980), but some films like *Badlands* (1973) or *Se7en* (1995) ultimately suggest the profound enigma of human psychopathology. *Natural Born Killers* (1994) suggests that while violence may be morally inexplicable, it is also shaped and intensified by its representation in the media. If many crime stories express our fascination with transgression but ultimately soothe our fears by restoring social order (for evil must be mapped and understood), some films – like *Se7en* – offer troubling exceptions. As we will see in chapter four, the serial killer's intrinsic anonymity and illegibility in the city both prompts and reflects profound social anxiety about modernity, and these anxieties are not assuaged, even when the killer may die, as John Doe (Kevin Spacey) does at the end of *Se7en*.

Thomas Leitch suggests that the crime film foregrounds the categories of criminal, investigator and crime, and that there is a continual breakdown and re-establishment of the borders between these categories (2002: 1–17). Rather than taking a strict chronological approach, the following chapters will follow Leitch's categories, with the last two chapters focusing on the criminal. Naturally, these categories present overlapping areas, as *The Silence of the Lambs* and *Se7en* can emphasise both the psychology of the criminal (Hannibal Lecter, John Doe) and a narrative enigma (the detective must solve a crime or prevent the next crime from occurring). Although the primary focus of this study will be on films about murder, our discussion will also include other crimes, including robbery (the heist film) and corruption and fraud (the police procedural, the courtroom drama).

Let us take a look at some of the key elements of the mystery or detective story from which crime films are often adapted. As many crime stories deal with narrative enigmas that involve questions relating to a crime – who did it? why? how? (and sometimes when and where?) – *hermeneutics*, or the process of *reading and interpreting* the crime scene, as if it were a text, is a central narrative issue (see Glossary). Crime stories have a special kind of narrative structure, which Roland Barthes calls 'teleological', or, like a strip tease, which points forward to its ending and to the solution of certain narrative questions (1975: 10). Edgar Allan Poe (1809–49) suggested that mystery writers first write their plots backwards, because he believed that crime fiction should emulate the structure and precision of mathematical formulae. Crime narratives operate on two levels; on the one hand, they tell the story of the crime, but simultaneously they also tell the story of its investigation (Todorov 1977: 44–5). They feature recurrent formal elements of temporal displacement (such as flashbacks), causality, delay and suspense (Pyrhönen 1994). The *mise-en-scène* of crime films may represent space as labyrinthine and knowledge/vision as partial, to which both the detective's and spectator's interpretative skills must be applied. Crime investigations, like criminal trials, emphasise storytelling or the transformation of inchoate data, evidence and clues into narratives with closure (we want to learn who killed the victim, and why). Through its fragmented narratives the crime story invites the active participation of the reader/viewer, prompting a desire, along with the detective, or jury, to know and understand. Ultimately, the character of the detective is a fantasy response to the anxiety provoked by crime's transgression, restoring social order and moral certainty by solving the crime. Like the all-seeing-eye advertising logo of the Pinkerton Detective agency (with the motto, 'We never sleep', founded in 1850 and later the first national private detective agency) the detective offers omniscient vision and narrative control, and embodies the logic and reason needed to interpret and solve crime.

Historical changes in criminal justice and investigation

Population changes, migration, wars and other social disruptions have transformed criminal investigation and policing. In medieval Europe, criminals were branded with a distinctive identifying mark. With the physical and social mobility and rapid urbanisation enabled by the Industrial Revolution, people moved from their small rural communities to the anonymous spaces of cities where traditional markers like language, class, accent, behaviour and dress were no longer reliable means of social identification. With the formation of the early-modern state, European societies became increasingly interested in controlling and identifying social populations. Changes in ideas about the cause of crime and the purposes of punishment brought about new demands for forms of criminal identification, in order to track and control recidivist (or repeat) offenders. The institutionalisation of the police force and various penal reforms in the nineteenth century began in England with the London Metropolitan Police Act of 1829, which established police officers, also known as 'bobbies' or 'peelers' (named after Sir Robert Peel, the Home Secretary) as the first municipal force in the world to walk regular beats to deter crime. England was soon followed by the US with Boston (1837) and New York (1845) Police Departments.

In the nineteenth century various pseudo-scientific ideas emerged which linked race, criminality and genetics, with the most influential being eugenics, which held that criminality was innate and signified by certain external physical features such as large or small craniums, high foreheads, large ears and other physical variants. Eugenics built on the medieval belief of *physiognomy* (see Glossary), which assumed that personality was inscribed on the physical body (especially the face), and also connected to *phrenology*, which held that a person's inner character was readable through the exterior shape of their cranial bones. Based on the writings of Swiss physician Johann Lavater (*Essays on Physiognomy*, 1775–78) and Italian criminologist Cesare Lombroso (*Criminal Man*, 1876) eugenics divided human beings into genetic and racial hierarchies in which non-white populations, the mentally ill, the poor and the working classes were genetically inferior to upper-class Anglo-Saxons. Influenced by these ideas, Alphonse Bertillon (1853–1914) the director of the Service de l'Identité Judicaire in Paris, developed a new criminological identification system, called *anthropometry* (see Glossary). This consisted of eleven detailed measurements of specific parts of a criminal's body, such as the length of the arm bone, the shape of the ear, and so on, which were combined with a new photographic and descriptive system for characterising offenders. Bertillon developed this system so that the police could use it to identify repeat criminal offenders and keep track of their identities and offences. Bertillon's profile and frontal photographs of offenders or *portraits parlés*

Fig. 1 Mapping the criminal body: Alphonse Bertillon, designer of the first criminal identification system

('speaking likenesses') were the first bureaucratic mug shots. He used the profile shot because of his belief that the shape of the ear was a distinctive identifier, and this remains a convention to this day in police mug shots. First adopted by the Paris police in 1883, by the 1890s the Bertillon system had been widely adopted in police departments around the world, but would eventually be replaced by fingerprint identification.

The end of the Bertillon system came with an unusual case of iden-tification. In 1903, a man named Will West was arrested and sent to Fort Leavenworth in Kansas, where it turned out another man, also named

William West was already imprisoned, and whose photographs and Bertillon measurements were identical to the first Will West. Fingerprints success-fully identified each man correctly (the two were subsequently believed to be identical twins). Despite the overthrow of Bertillon's system of bodily measurements as inaccurate and bureaucratically cumbersome, his other contributions like the mug shot and the systematisation of crime-scene photography remain in place to this day. Fingerprints, or *dactyloscopy* (see Glossary), emerged at the same time as Bertillonage, developed by a number of British colonial officials including Sir William Herschel, Henry Faulds and Sir Francis Galton, whose book *Fingerprints* (1892) became the first fingerprint classification system. In Argentina in 1892, Juan Vucetich became the first police officer in the world to solve a case by fingerprints, proving that a woman named Rojas had murdered her two sons through the bloody print she left on a door. In 1900, the British Belper Committee exam-ined the competing claims of anthropometry and fingerprints as identifica-tion systems, and recommended the adoption of the latter. Between 1902 and 1905 various American state, federal and military authorities adopted fingerprint identification methods. In 1910, Thomas Jennings became the first person in the US convicted because of fingerprint evidence. In 1972, fingerprints became retrievable by computer, and eventually became part of the Automated Fingerprint Identification System (AFIS).

Today DNA has become an important new tool in law enforcement. Unlike fingerprints, DNA is an identification system based on probability, rather than uniqueness, and is therefore called DNA *profiling*, rather than identification. Today, matching a person's DNA in their blood, sweat, saliva, tears, semen or skin to trace evidence at the scene of the crime can con-vict them. In 1988, in the UK, Colin Pitchfork became the first person in the world to be convicted of murder based on DNA evidence. In 1994, the first American states began establishing a genetic identification database, now called the Combined DNA Identification System (CODIS) which like AFIS receives frequent mention on the television drama *CSI*. Since the violent events of 11 September 2001, customs, immigration and law enforcement agencies in the US increasingly use *biometrics* (see Glossary) as a means of visual identification to prevent terrorism, while the UK uses an extensive network of CCTV (Closed Circuit Television) cameras.

From Bertillonage to dactyloscopy, and from DNA to biometrics, insti-tutions continue to use new technologies in order to discipline, map and control the criminal body. The central role which some of these technologies play on television crime shows are only the most recent development of the crime story, to the history of which we now turn.

Historical origins of the crime story

Centuries before the stories of Arthur Conan Doyle and Edgar Allan Poe, other cultures had versions of the crime story. For example, China had a long tradition of the judicial detective story, like the stories of Pu Songling (1640–1715), which featured protagonists who were district magistrates or judges. In these stories the judge usually had to solve three, sometimes interlocking, crimes, which often included supernatural elements (such as ghosts of the victims). Unlike the Western detective story, the identity of the criminal was known from the start, and the narrative's focus was on unravelling the means and motive of the crime, rather than identifying and capturing the guilty suspect.

Appearing in England in five volumes beginning around 1773, an antecedent of the crime story was *The Newgate Calendar*. Published by the chaplain of Newgate prison, it featured the confessions and last words of the condemned before execution. Many other imitators followed, including *The Malefactor's Register* (1779) and *Criminal Chronology* (1809). In the United States, the execution sermon first made an appearance in the late seventeenth century, and focused on the spiritual state of the condemned before execution, rather than on the crime, or the trial; prison crime dramas like *Dead Man Walking* (1995) and *The Green Mile* (1999) are modern variants of this tradition. The execution sermon portrayed the criminal as a sinner, with whom readers were encouraged to identify, as fellow sinners. This is a radical difference from later crime stories of the eighteenth and nineteenth centuries which, by contrast, promoted the reader's horror and disgust with the crime, and which depicted the criminal as someone fundamentally alien (Halttunen 1998: 3).

The American and British crime film has its origins in late nineteenth-century developments in Western crime literature, which emerged from several different literary strands: the gothic novel, sensationalist fiction and theatre, and the emergence of the detective story in Britain, France and the US. The Gothic story was characterised by three seminal English novels: Horace Walpole's *The Castle of Otranto: A Gothic Story* (1764), Ann

Radcliffe's *The Mysteries of Udolpho* (1794) and Matthew Lewis's *The Monk* (1796). Gothic novels featured macabre and supernatural tales, and were usually set in haunted castles, wild landscapes, ruined houses or grave-yards. As Fred Botting describes it, 'spectres, monsters, demons, corpses, skeletons, evil aristocrats, monks and nuns, fainting heroines and bandits populate Gothic landscapes' and were joined in the nineteenth century by 'scientists, fathers, husbands, madmen, criminals, and the monstrous double' (1996: 2). The Gothic novel's mysterious, sublime or horrific stories were meant to terrify and amaze the reader, and influenced nineteenth-century works like Mary Shelley's *Frankenstein* (1818), Charlotte Brönte's *Jane Eyre* (1847) and Emily Brönte's *Wuthering Heights* (1847), Robert Louis Stevenson's *The Strange Case of Dr Jekyll and Mr Hyde* (1886) and Bram Stoker's *Dracula* (1897). The crime film would borrow Gothic literature's violent and macabre elements, its atmosphere of terror and suspense, and like the horror film, sometimes its supernatural and uncanny elements. Many Gothic novels were subsequently adapted to film and form part of the film cycle of crime or Gothic melodramas like *Rebecca* (1940), the British version of *Gaslight* (1940, aka *Angel Street*) and its American counterpart *Gaslight* (1944) (see Barefoot 2001). The Gothic tradition continues to be an important source for many crime and horror films today, as with *Bram Stoker's Dracula* (1992) and *Mary Shelley's Frankenstein* (1994).

Around 1800, developments in forensic medicine led to the first pub-lished accounts of postmortems. These accounts also influenced a key ele-ment of the crime story and, later, crime film: the importance of body horror. At the same time that changes in Victorian social practices meant that the body became progressively absent from the public sphere, crime stories increasingly focused on graphic details like corporeal putrefaction, echo-ing Gothic literature's ambivalent fascination and repulsion with the body. With the expansion of newspaper publishing and improvements in literacy and education in the nineteenth century, crime became a staple subject of journalism. At their popular height between 1860 and 1910, American dime novels were a new marketing phenomenon which expanded readership by making cheap paperbacks for a nickel or dime widely available, partially overlapping with the birth of pulp fiction magazines like *Argosy*, *Detective Fiction*, *Detective Story* and *Dime Detective Crimebusters*, which began appearing in the 1880s. Dime novels and pulp magazines specialised in westerns, crime stories and action and adventure tales, and helped popularise two heroic protagonists of crime fiction and, later, film: the sheriff, deputy or US Marshal, and the police officer or private eye. In Britain in the 1860s a new literary cycle of sensationalism emerged, with novels and plays, often based on real-life crimes of passion that increasingly received coverage in the newspapers of the period. Unlike the Gothic novel, sensationalism marked a shift into the everyday world, emblematised by Wilkie Collins' *The Woman in White* (1860, first filmed in 1912 in two silent versions), Mrs H. Wood's *East Lynne* (1861) and Mary Elizabeth Braddon's *Lady Audley's Secret* (1862).

Influenced by the Gothic and sensational genres, the nineteenth century saw the emergence and development of the Western detective story. In three seminal stories 'The Murders in the Rue Morgue' (1841), 'The Mystery of Marie Roget' (1842–43) and 'The Purloined Letter' (1845), Edgar Allan Poe introduced C. Auguste Dupin, the classic detective who became the forerunner of all other amateur sleuths. In fact 'The Murders in the Rue Morgue' established a number of canonical features of the classical detective story or whodunit: the incompetence of the police in comparison to the amateur detective; the sensational crime in an (apparently) locked room; a trail of false clues left by the murderer; an atmosphere of creepy suspense; the unexpected solution of the crime; and the guilt of the most unlikely suspect (which in 'The Murders in the Rue Morgue' turns out to be a runaway orangutan). The three Dupin stories also initiated the convention of the detective's assistant/friend who chronicles or narrates the story, and which anticipated Sherlock Holmes' Watson, Hercule Poirot's Captain Hastings and Philo Vance's narrator, S. S. Van Dine (pseudonym for Willard Huntington Wright).

After Poe, the detective genre gained popularity with Anna Katharine Green's *The Leavenworth Case* (1878) and Mary Roberts Rinehart's *The Circular Staircase* (1908) in America; Wilkie Collins, Arthur Conan Doyle and G. K. Chesterton in England; and Gaston Leroux, Eugène Sue and Emile Gaboriau in France. Master criminal prototypes like Honoré de Balzac's Ferragus (*Histoire des Treize*) and Vautrin (*Père Goriot*), along with Conan Doyle's Professor Moriarty, were modelled on real-life figures such as French master thief Eugene Vidocq (1775–1857), and would later find their cinematic equivalent in Fritz Lang's Dr Mabuse, and Louis Feuillade's Judex, Irma Vep and Fantômas. By the twentieth century the detective story and classical whodunit was in full flourish, with the era between the end of the

First World War and 1939 known as the Golden Age of Detective Fiction. 1920 was a seminal year for the detective story, which saw the publication of British author Agatha Christie's *The Mysterious Affairs at Styles* and Irish author Freeman Wills Crofts' *The Cask*, with the Americans joining the detective genre with S. S. Van Dine's *The Benson Murder Case* in 1926. Many of their stories would be adapted into the classic whodunit film that is discussed further in chapter one.

'Torn from the Headlines': the crime film and its social context

From a bank robber shooting directly into the camera in Edwin S. Porter's *The Great Train Robbery* (1903) to *Sherlock Holmes Baffled* (1900–3), early filmmakers made crime a compelling subject for cinema. French director Ferdinand Zecca's short *Histoire d'un crime* (*History of a Crime*, 1901) showed a crime of passion and the murderer's subsequent execution on the guillotine, exemplifying two key elements of the crime film: the commission of the crime and its subsequent punishment. Early films which treated crime as a social and moral issue included *The Ex-Convict* (1904), a story about a man released from prison who is driven to commit crime in response to social ostracism and poverty, and *The Kleptomaniac* (1905) in which rich and poor thieves are treated differently. Crime was often a subject for spectacle, with innovative camera placement and editing in *The Great Train Robbery* offering the spectator an intimate vision of violent death (Sklar 2002: 38). In the 1910s as cinema developed in both narrative length and formal complexity, filmmakers turned to popular crime fiction and accounts of real-life crime 'torn from the headlines' for source material, and many studios began to make serials, or short films, with multiple installments and cliffhanger endings.

French Director Louis Feuillade's *Fantômas* was one of the earliest crime serials (1913–14). Based on the serials of Marcel Allain and Pierre Souvestre, *Fantômas* began with a story of the eponymous master-criminal (played by René Navarre) seducing a woman and murdering her husband, while matching wits with police Inspector Juve (Edmond Bréon). It was followed by *Les Vampires* (1915–16), a serial in ten parts, about a gang of jewel thieves led by the incomparable Irma Vep (an anagram of 'vampire') who prowled the rooftops of Paris sheathed in black. Playing the wicked Vep was the actress Musidora, who returned as the evil Diana Monti in *Judex* (1916–17), in its sequel *The New Mission of Judex* (1917) and finally in her own series *Tih Minh* (1918). All of these Feuillade serials featured highly intelligent criminals or vigilante figures that would prefigure later superheroes like Batman or Zorro. Praised by the Surrealists for their visual style and striking photography of the Parisian cityscape, these serials were enormously popular with the public, offering them a blend of the erotic thriller, crime story and melodrama. In the US *The Monogrammed Cigarette* (1910) marked a new series, which included *The Woman Who Dared* (1911), and which was unusual for featuring a female investigator, 'daughter to a famous detective', and which anticipated the female heroines of later adventure serials like *The Perils of Pauline* (1914) and *The Exploits of Elaine* (1914–15) (see Bowser 1990: 185).

Another important influence in the Anglo-American crime film was through two traditions in German cinema. Influenced by the visual style and dark psychological themes of Expressionism (see Glossary) in the late 1910s and early 1920s, German cinema had a strong tradition of fantasy, drawing stories from national legends, myths, or fairytales like *Der Student von Prague* (*The Student of Prague*, 1913), *Der Golem* (*The Golem*, 1920) and *Nosferatu* (1922), while an alternative realist tradition of Strassenfilme or 'street films' examined poverty, unemployment and prostitution in Karl Grune's *Die Strasse* (*The Street*, 1923) or G. W. Pabst's *Die Freudlose Gasse* (*Joyless Street*, 1925). Whether fantastic or realist, many German films featured crime and murderers like Caligari in Robert Weine's *Das Cabinet des Dr Caligari* (*The Cabinet of Dr Caligari*, 1919) or psychopaths like the Jack the Ripper figure in *Die Büchse der Pandora* (*Pandora's Box*, 1929) and Peter Lorre's serial killer and paedophile in Fritz Lang's *M* (1931). In the 1920s Lang made a series of crime thrillers focusing on the underworld and master criminals, including the eponymous *Dr Mabuse the Gambler*, in two parts, and *Das Testament des Dr Mabuse* (*The Testament of Dr Mabuse*, 1933), as well as *Die Spinnen* (*Spiders*, 1919) and *Spione* (*Spies*, 1928). Dr Mabuse exemplified the criminal mastermind through his wraith-like ability to infiltrate ordinary society, his mastery of disguises, his uncanny hypnotic powers, and his superior intellectual ability (always outwitting the police and other governmental agents). As we will see in chapter four, Lang's criminal mastermind would influence later criminal portraits like the serial killer John Doe in *Se7en* or Hannibal Lecter in *The Silence of the Lambs*.

Crime films and the coming of sound

As Ian Cameron has emphasised, 'no genre has been more consistently shaped by factors outside the cinema than the crime movie'. He goes on to suggest that the crime genre 'demands to be seen in the context of actual crime, and consistently refers to identifiable people, events or situations' (1975: 12). D. W. Griffith's *Musketeers of Pig Alley* (1912) fictionalised the Lower East Side tenements of New York City, which teemed with immigrants and juvenile gangs, and also alluded to Jacob Riis's famous photographic study *How the Other Half Lives* (1890). Exploitation films like *Traffic in Lost Souls* (1913) and *Inside the White Slave Traffic* (1913) capitalised on sensational topics and ostensible social problems like enforced (white) prostitution, then receiving extensive newspaper coverage. Other social concerns about police corruption, street crime and high immigration would later find their way into early gangster films, as *Musketeers of Pig Alley* was rapidly followed by Raoul Walsh's *Regeneration* (1915), Maurice Tourneur's *Alias Jimmy Valentine* (1915), Josef Von Sternberg's *Underworld* (1927) and Lewis Milestone's *The Racket* (1928). Many of these films were 'torn from the headlines' with the story for *Underworld* and the screenplay for *Scarface* written by a journalist, Ben Hecht. The coming of sound brought new genres to American cinema, from the romantic screwball comedy to the Busby Berkeley musical, and new twists on old genres, with the gangster film now featuring the squealing of tyres, the sputter of machine guns and gritty urban patois. In fact, the first American sound film *Lights of New York* (1928) was a gangster film (*The Jazz Singer* (1927) was only partially recorded in sound).

But it was the real-life bloody exploits of gang warfare between Al Capone and his rivals which made the front pages of all the national American newspapers. With the onset of Prohibition with the Volstead Act (see Glossary) of 1918, which banned the consumption and distribution of alcohol between 1919 and 1933, criminal organisations with specific ethnic identities (Irish, Italian, Jewish) rapidly moved into the business of providing illegal liquor to Americans. Meanwhile, crime dramas were popular in theatre (*The Last Mile*, 1930) and newspaper and radio series (*Calling All Cars*, 1933–39). In the early 1930s, stars like James Cagney (*The Public Enemy*, *The Roaring Twenties* (1939)) and Edward G. Robinson (*Little Caesar*, *Bullets or Ballots* (1936)) became strongly associated with the gangster genre through a

Fig. 2 Mug shot of notorious gangster Al Capone (1899–1947), taken in 1931 on his arrest for tax evasion

series of iconic roles. Similarly, although later known for his tough good guy roles of the 1940s, Humphrey Bogart began his career as a gangster in *Bullets or Ballots, The Petrified Forest* (1936) and *Kid Galahad* (1937).

The release of *Little Caesar, The Public Enemy* and *Scarface* in the early 1930s institutionalised the gangster genre in American cinema. Limited by the demands of the Production or Hays Code (see Glossary), which became more rigorously enforced in 1934, crime films could not show (in any detail) the commission or execution of a crime, or show criminals succeeding in a criminal enterprise. Under these constraints, the gangster genre became a tragic tale of hubris, in which the gangster had to be destroyed or imprisoned in order for social order to be restored. Consequently, by the end of each film, viewers saw the gangster as a corpse in *The Public Enemy*, or dying in a hail of bullets in *The Roaring Twenties*, or exclaiming, as does Rico Bandello (Edward G. Robinson) in *Little Caesar*: 'Mother of God, is this the end of Rico?'

With the onset of the Depression and its widespread poverty and high unemployment, real-life American robbers and killers like Machine Gun Kelly, Baby Face Nelson, Ma Barker, Pretty Boy Floyd and Bonnie Parker and Clyde Barrow became celebrity outlaws, who, in the public imagination, robbed from the rich (the banks, the tycoons) and gave to the poor, and

Fig. 3 Criminal folk heroes
Bonnie Parker and Clyde Barrow

whose exciting exploits were eagerly followed by the public on the front pages of newspapers and in newsreels. The romantic roots of the crime film can be traced back to legends and ballads about British outlaws like Dick Turpin, together with songs and dime-store novels about American outlaws of the Wild West like Jessie James and Billy the Kid. The legends around these men quickly transferred to the working-class heroes of Dillinger, Parker and Clyde. Ironically, in 1934 John Dillinger met a suitably cinematic end, as police gunned him down after he went to see a screening of the gangster film *Manhattan Melodrama* at the Biograph theatre in Chicago. Many of these outlaws were fictionalised in the American gangster genre of the 1930s, and again in an exploitation cycle from the late 1950s to the end of the 1960s, with biopics like *Baby Face Nelson* (1957), *Machine Gun Kelly* (1958), *Al Capone* (1959), *The Rise and Fall of Legs Diamond* (1960), *The George Raft Story* (1961), *Bonnie and Clyde* (1967) and *Bloody Mama* (1970).

Like many gangster films of the period, *Doorway to Hell* (1930) and *The Roaring Twenties* were concerned with the social roots of crime, and films like *I Am a Fugitive from a Chain Gang* (1932), *Marked Woman* (1937), *Dead End* (aka *Cradle of Crime*, 1937) and *Angels With Dirty Faces* (1938) suggested that the roots of criminality lay in conditions of urban poverty and unemployment, with bootlegging and racketeering as career paths to success for first- and second-generation immigrants. Fictional characters like the street gangs and juvenile delinquents of the Bowery Boys and Dead End Kids spawned sequels and film cycles that lasted well into the 1940s. Building on his work in the western genre, Richard Slotkin describes the gangster as a twentieth-century development of the American frontier myth, in which the city was the new Wild West (1992: 260–5). The gangster film reflected the classic American success story of the Horatio Alger novels, in which a working-class boy pulls himself up by his own bootstraps and through his initiative and entrepreneurial drive becomes rich. As Tony Camonte (a fictionalised version of Al Capone, played here by Paul Muni) bluntly formulates it in *Scarface*: 'Do it first, do it yourself, and keep on doing it.' The gangster has a paradoxical appeal; on the one hand, he represents the forces of disorder and criminality, but at the same time he is also a charismatic criminal entrepreneur. As Robert Warshow describes it, 'the gangster is the "no" to that great American "yes" which is stamped so big over our official culture' (2002: 136). In other words, the gangster genre is the central paradigm for investigating the contradictions of the American dream, and as Glenn Man suggests, 'exposes the ruthlessness and greed that undergird the American system of capitalism' (2000: 109).

In 1924 the Bureau of Investigation, renamed the Federal Bureau of Investigation in 1935, began its long tenure under the leadership of J. Edgar Hoover, which would last until his death in 1972. By the mid-1930s Hollywood began to shift from the gangster film to a cycle of crime films like *G-Men* (1935) and *Bullets or Ballots*, which heroicised the FBI, and which returned again in the 1950s with *The FBI Story* (1959). FBI agent Elliot Ness's legendary fight against Al Capone was immortalised in *The Untouchables* television series (1959–63) and the later film of the same name (1987). As we discuss further in chapter four with *The Silence of the Lambs*, fifty years later the heroic federal agent would return, this time to use her training in behavioural psychology and criminal profiling to track down serial killers, not gangsters.

Along with the gangster genre, the prison film was another important type of crime film developed in the 1930s, and exemplified by *The Big House* (1930), *The Criminal Code* (1931) and *Each Dawn I Die* (1939). The prison film focused on the aftermath of crime, the punishment (and sometimes execution) of the criminal, the sadistic treatment of prisoners by each other, or by prison guards (*Brute Force* (1947)), or the prison break (*The Shawshank Redemption* (1994)). The prison crime story continues in television with series like *Porridge* (1974–77, UK), *Oz* (1997–2003, US), *Prisoner: Cell Block H* (1979–86, Australia) and *Prison Break* (2005–present, US). It is from the prison crime film that we get slang words like 'stoolie', 'shiv', 'porridge' and 'screw' (Maloney 1998).

The 1940s crime film

By World War Two the gangster genre had largely disappeared, replaced by the investigative narratives of the hard-boiled detectives of the 1940s (see chapter two), and by a series of spy thrillers in which crimes of espionage and sabotage reflected wartime concerns in films like *Saboteur* (1942), *The Mask of Dimitrios* (1943) and *The Stranger* (1946). The hard-boiled detective was the heroic investigator of a new type of crime fiction created by Raymond Chandler, Dashiell Hammett, James M. Cain and Mickey Spillane, amongst others, which was modernist and urban, largely set in the streets of New York, Los Angeles, San Francisco and Chicago. Appearing on the screen were stories by Cain (*Double Indemnity* (1944), *Mildred Pierce* (1945), *The Postman Always Rings Twice* (1946)); by Hammett (*The Maltese Falcon* (1931 and 1941), *The Thin Man* (1934) and sequels, (*The Glass Key* (1942)); and Chandler (*Murder, My Sweet* (1944), *The Big Sleep* (1946), *The Blue Dahlia* (1946), *Lady in the Lake* (1947), and the screenplay for *Double Indemnity*)). Hard-boiled literature was the source material for a cycle of low-budget crime films that would become known as *film noir* (see Glossary). Rather than the upper-class amateurs of the whodunit (see chapter one), the private eye is a working-class man, easily able to slip into the seedy underworld of prostitution, gambling and gangsters of the American city. Forty years before, in 'A Defence of Detective Stories' (first published in 1902), the creator of the *Father Brown* mystery stories, G. K. Chesterton, defended the detective story as a popular art form which showed the 'poetry of modern life'. He argued that the detective was an agent of 'social justice' that challenged what he called the original 'cosmic conservatives' (1946: 4). Raymond Chandler later supported Chesterton's claim for the essential modernity of the crime story. In his 1944 essay 'The Simple Art of Murder' Chandler observed of Dashiell Hammett that he 'took murder out of the Venetian vase and dropped it into the alley' (1944: 54). Changing the formula of the classic whodunit of Agatha Christie and Arthur Conan Doyle, he suggested that 'Hammett gave murder back to the kind of people who commit it for reasons, not just to provide a corpse; and with the means at hand, not with handwrought duelling pistols, curare and tropical fish' (ibid.).

In addition to the hard-boiled detective, film noir included other kinds of crime stories, such as boxing films (*Body and Soul* (1947) and *The Set-Up* (1947)); criminal couples on the lam (*Gun Crazy* (1949), *They Live By Night* (1949)); police procedurals (*The Naked City* (1948)); the heist film (*The Asphalt Jungle* (1950), *The Killing* (1956)); studies in sociopathy (*Kiss of Death* (1947), *White Heat*); and the woman's thriller (*Rebecca*). Cops were no longer the heroic FBI men of the 1930s' gangster genre, but accidental murderers like Detective Sgt. Mark Dixon (Dana Andrews) in *Where the Sidewalk Ends* (1950), or profoundly corrupt like Hank Quinlan (Orson Welles) in *Touch of Evil* (1958). Youth culture, motorcycle gangs and drug addiction became new subjects for the crime film, with *East of Eden* (1955), *Rebel Without a Cause* (1955), *Blackboard Jungle* (1955) and *The Wild One* (1955). The world of crime was no longer a separate realm and being in one's car (*The Hitch-hiker* (1953)), house (*Desperate Hours* (1955)), or simply innocent (*The Wrong Man* (1956)), did not protect citizens from the criminal world.

Postwar developments

Whereas the gangster genre and other crime films of the 1940s focused on the individual criminal and their relationship to the underworld, by the 1950s crime became a metaphor for institutional corruption, and the gangster had become a corporate man. As Jonathan Munby suggests, the separation of law enforcement and the criminal underworld in the 1930s gangster film had by the 1950s become a bleak portrait of all-pervasive corruption and graft (1999: 133). In 1950–51, the US Senate's Special Committee to Investigate Organised Crime in Interstate Commerce Hearings (the Kefauver Commission) began an investigation into the existence and influence of the American Mafia in American business, government and trade (which would later be alluded to in Francis Ford Coppola's *Godfather II* (1974)). Together with the later McClellan Committee of the 1960s, the Kefauver Commission looked at interstate gambling and racketeering, and in 1957 confirmed the existence of the Mafia and its leadership, describing the ways in which the Mob hid its criminal activity through money laundering practices and business fronts. *The Enforcer* (1951) first took up these subjects, and was quickly followed by *The Mob* (1951), *The Racket* (1951), *The Captive City* (1952), *On the Waterfront* (1954), *The Phenix City Story* (1955), *The Big Combo* (1955), *The Killers* (1964) and *Point Blank* (1967). The Kefauver Commission led to new law enforcement tools and legislation, which later included the Witness Security and Protection Program (WITSEC) and the Racketeer Influence and Corrupt Organisations (RICO) Act, both established in 1970. Finally, by the early 1970s, the publication of three bestsellers (each of which would subsequently be adapted to film), returned the Italian gangster to the public imagination: Peter Maas's *The Valachi Papers* (novel, 1968; film 1972), Gay Talese's *Honor Thy Father* (novel 1971, TV film 1973) and Mario Puzo's *The Godfather* (novel 1969, film 1972).

In 1968 the American Production Code (see Glossary) was replaced by the MPAA Ratings system, which now classified films according to age-appropriate content, introducing G, PG, PG-13, R and later NC-17 ratings. Because of their violent content crime films generally attract R ratings (restricted to persons over 17, unless accompanied by an adult) or NC-17 (no-one admitted under 17). The Production Code had long restricted the content of crime films, the representation of violence and the characterisation of criminals, and with its end, new genres and forms of the crime story were now possible. For example, the caper or heist film of the late 1960s, in which criminals successfully got away with the proceeds of their crimes, could not have occurred under the rules of the Production Code, which stated that 'theft, robbery, safe-cracking and dynamiting of trains, mines, buildings etc should not be detailed in method', nor could criminal Hannibal Lecter (Anthony Hopkins) be shown about to eat his former tormentor at the end of *The Silence of The Lambs*. Cops could now be heroic rogues (*Dirty Harry* (1971)) and citizens could be vigilantes (*Death Wish* (1974)). Changes in special effects led to new standards of realism, with the use of squibs in *Bonnie and Clyde* and later *The Godfather* realistically showing the effects of machine gun bullets on the human body (as when Sonny Corleone (James Caan) is assassinated). *Bonnie and Clyde* was a seminal film, not just for its groundbreaking realism in the depiction of violence, but also for its comical tone which celebrated the eponymous outlaws as anti-establishment heroes. Like the work of many directors of the New American Cinema that emerged in the late 1960s and early 1970s, Arthur Penn's film is a self-conscious look at the relationship between crime and celebrity and popular culture. As Clyde says to Bonnie in response to a poem she wrote about their exploits, 'You made me somebody they're going to remember.' Twenty-seven years later Oliver Stone's film *Natural Born Killers* would also examine the relationship between the media and crime. In the 1960s and 1970s new films like *Psycho*, *The Wild Bunch*, *Dirty Harry*, *A Clockwork Orange*, *Frenzy* (1972) and *Taxi Driver* (1976) showed heroic criminals, graphic and sadistic violence, and other formerly-taboo subjects, and influenced by social changes in which rebellion, transgression and sexual freedom were now celebrated, the face of the crime film would be forever changed.

In 1968 three rogue cop films – *Bullitt*, *Madigan* and *Coogan's Bluff* – showed the transgressive turn the police film would take in the 1970s with *Dirty Harry*, *The French Connection* (1971), *Walking Tall* (1973) and *Death Wish*, which is discussed further in chapter two. These films appealed to rising social concerns about American urban crime, as well as the corruption unveiled in Watergate. After a decade in which the gangster film had largely disappeared (with the exception of *The Brotherhood* (1968)), *The Godfather* and *Mean Streets* (1973) marked the return of the genre, which would proliferate in the 1980s, 1990s and 2000s with the continuing work of Martin Scorsese (*Goodfellas* (1990), *Casino* (1995), *Gangs of New York* (2002) and *The Departed* (2006)). New variants in the gangster genre appeared, with ethnic gangs from Chinese tongs (*Year of the Dragon* (1985)) to the Russian Mafia (*Romeo is Bleeding* (1993), (*Little Odessa* (1994)), to the yakuza genre (*Violent Cop* (1989)). The *Godfather* trilogy (1972–1990) became a part of American popular culture and influenced later television shows like *The Sopranos* (see Browne 2000: 1–22). In the early 1990s a new type of crime film sometimes called the 'hood' or 'gangsta' film emerged with a cycle of African-American films about inner-city violence in the work of Spike Lee (*Do the Right Thing* (1989), *Clockers* (1995)); John Singleton (*Boyz N the Hood* (1991)) Matty Rice (*Straight Out of Brooklyn* (1991)); Mario Van Peebles (*New Jack City* (1991)); Ernest Dickerson (*Juice* (1991)); and Allen and Albert Hughes (*Menace II Society* (1993); *Dead Presidents* (1995)) (see Massood 2003). In the 1980s and 1990s, wealthy businessmen like Gordon Gekko in *Wall Street* (1987) with his mantra of 'greed is good' became the new criminal villains (see also *A Perfect Murder* (1998) and *The Player* (1992)). Beginning with *Henry: Portrait of a Serial Killer* and *Manhunter* (1986) and proliferating in the next two decades (*The Silence of the Lambs*, *Copycat* (1995), *Citizen X* (1995), *Suspect Zero* (2004)), the serial killer film presented a new kind of criminal anti-hero, from the baroquely Gothic (Hannibal Lecter) to the fanatically evil (John Doe). Meanwhile auteurs like Quentin Tarantino and the Coen brothers formed part of a broader movement that burlesqued or reinvented classic forms of the crime film, using postmodern techniques of pastiche (see Glossary) and citation. Like Tarantino's *Pulp Fiction* (1994) or the Coen brothers' noir comedy *Fargo* (1995), these films are playful in tone, irreverent in their depiction of graphic violence, and eclectic and self-reflexive in their play with generic conventions.

Meanwhile, in the UK, between 1997 and 2001, 25 British gangster films were released, surpassing the total number of the previous two decades. The commercial success of Guy Ritchie's *Lock, Stock and Two Smoking Barrels* (1998) and *Snatch* (2000) followed earlier crime entries *The Long Good Friday*, *The Hit* (1984), *Mona Lisa* (1986), *The Krays* (1990), *Hard Men* (1996) and *Face* (1997), and was followed by *Sexy Beast* (2000) and *Layer Cake* (2004). Blending comic exaggeration and melodrama, Ritchie's films modelled themselves on three seminal British crime films: *The Italian Job* (1969), *Performance* (1970) and *Get Carter* (1971). Unlike the social reality of British crime which largely consisted of drug trafficking, car theft, counterfeiting and VAT manipulation, British crime films remained nostalgic stories of protection rackets, armed robbery, money laundering, betting and boxing. These films had a sharp ear for colourful vernacular and a flippant tone influenced by Tarantino, one-dimensional characterisations and stylised performances. With soundtracks which blended retro hits and chic club music, and narratives which foregrounded the homosocial bonds between men, the marketing of these films also targetted male consumers for their video rental or purchase (Chibnall 2001: 1–7). Many of these continued to feature the quasi-criminal character of the 'spiv' or a supplier of goods from dubious sources (Murphy 1993: 81–91), who first appeared in a postwar cycle of films (*Brighton Rock* (1947), *Night and the City* (1950)). In fact, 26 per cent of all crime films released between 1930 and 1983 were murder mysteries and thrillers (Gifford 1986: 12). Later cycles of British crime films included the gritty location shooting of the New Wave of the 1950s and beyond (*Hell is a City* (1959), *Payroll* (1961)), which also saw record numbers of B crime films released, and the comic heist films of the 1960s (*Gambit* (1966), *Deadfall* (1968)) (Chibnall & Murphy 1999: 1–15).

Crime auteurs: Alfred Hitchcock and others

One of the film directors most closely associated with the crime genre is British filmmaker Alfred Hitchcock (1899–1980), who, in the words of his own marketing slogan, was 'the master of suspense'. Hitchcock made 53 films, nearly all of them crime films, between 1926 and 1976, working in Germany, the UK and the US. Under the broad rubric of crime Hitchcock was a master of its many genres and sub-genres including the spy thriller (*Saboteur*, *The Secret Agent* (1936), *Notorious* (1946)); psychological thriller (*Suspicion* (1941), *Dial M for Murder* (1954)); woman's melodrama (*Rebecca*); courtroom drama (*The Paradine Case* (1948)); and stories of criminal psychopathology (*Shadow of a Doubt* (1943), *Rope*, *Strangers on a Train* (1951), *Psycho*, *Frenzy*; and the innocent man on the run (*The 39 Steps* (1935), *The Wrong Man*).

Influenced by the themes of madness and entrapment and the visual style of German Expressionism, as well as the gritty urban realism of the Weimar street film, Hitchcock's *The Lodger* (1926) was the second film adaptation of Marie Belloc Lowndes' story of Jack the Ripper, after *Waxworks* (1924) and before *Pandora's Box*. Hitchcock's films were extra-ordinarily influential in the evolution of the British and American crime film because of his technical mastery, original style and violation of narrative and generic conventions (which included killing off the main protagonist in *Psycho* and a false flashback in *Stage Fright* (1950)). Hitchcock's films were innovative in the use of subjective and non-naturalistic sound (*Blackmail* (1929), *Murder!* (1930) and sound montage (*The 39 Steps*); in Eisensteinian montage (*Psycho*, *Vertigo* (1958)); in his mastery of the long take, camera and widescreen (*Rope*); and in his manipulation of the spectator and thematic foregrounding of psychological aberrancy and voyeurism. He was a master of the chase sequence, frequently using the double chase, where an inno cent man is pursued by both criminals and the police (*The 39 Steps*). Many of his films featured spectacular chase sequences across public monuments like the Statue of Liberty in *Saboteur* or Mount Rushmore in *North by Northwest* (1959). Hitchcock's subversive view of criminality and innocence showed how an ordinary person could be tempted to commit murder

(*Blackmail*, *Strangers on a Train*) and how the everyday world could turn nightmarish (*The Birds* (1963)). Perhaps his greatest film was *Vertigo* (1958), a story about Scottie (James Stewart), a former police detective, whose obsession with two women, Madeleine and Judy (Kim Novak) – who ultimately turn out to be the same person – is ultimately a necrophilic study of obsession.

Another important figure in the crime film is Martin Scorsese, whose work has explored the Italian-American mafia (*Mean Streets*, *Casino*, *Goodfellas*), the nature of psychosis and vigilantism (*Taxi Driver*), and the historical relationship of New York City (*Gangs of New York*) or Boston (*The Departed*) to gangsterism. Other key crime auteurs include Don Siegel, who made a series of key films in the late 1960s and early 1970s (*Coogan's Bluff*, *Madigan*, *Dirty Harry*, *Charley Varrick* (1973)), and Sidney Lumet, whose crime tetralogy (*Serpico* (1973), *Q & A* (1980), *Prince of the City* (1981) and *Night Falls on Manhattan* (1987)) explored the issue of police corruption. Working in both film and television, Michael Mann is an important contemporary filmmaker who has refined the crime story, working on television cop series like *Miami Vice* (1984–89), *Crime Story* (1986–88) and *Robbery Homicide* (2002–03) and crime films like *Heat* (1995), *Collateral* (2004) and *Miami Vice* (2006). Finally, many other auteurs of the crime story have been writers and producers of innovative American television series, including Jerry Bruckheimer, the executive producer for *Without a Trace* (2002–present), *Cold Case* (2003–present) and *Justice* (2006–present), and *CSI* and its spin-offs; David E. Kelley, writer, producer or creator of *LA Law* (1986–94), *Ally McBeal* (1997–2002), *The Practice* (1997–2004), *Boston Legal* (2004–present) and *The Law Firm* (2005); and Steven Bochco, writer, story editor or executive producer on *Columbo* (pilot 1969, series 1971–78, intermittent 1998–2003), *McMillan and Wife* (1971–76), *Richie Brockelman; Private Eye* (1978), *Hill Street Blues* (1981–87), *Cop Rock* (1990), *NYPD Blue* (1993–2005), *Murder One* (1995–97), *Philly* (2001–02), *Blind Justice* (2005) and *Hollis and Rae* (2006).

Chapter one of this study, 'Crime as Puzzle', takes a look at three important types of crime story in which the crime's execution or solution must be decoded: the whodunit, the forensic drama *CSI* and the heist film. The whodunit or murder mystery featured amateur sleuths like Sherlock Holmes, Hercule Poirot or Miss Marple, who approached the crime as an intellectual puzzle to be solved through a mixture of specialised knowledge and common-sense. Like the classic whodunit, the television show *CSI* also depicts crime as a puzzle, and invites the viewer to solve the case through forensic evidence and the aid of science. We will also look at the heist film, which offers the viewer the vicarious pleasures of the planning and execution of a difficult or complicated crime, such as safe-cracking.

While chapter one focuses on the crime and its investigation by amateur sleuths, chapter two, 'The Professional Crime Solver', turns to the private eye, policeman, federal agent or lawyer. We trace changes in the police officer, from the crime-fighting heroes of 1930s gangster films, to the rogue cops of the 1970s, and also look at television from *Dragnet* to present-day dramas (*Law and Order*), reality-based shows (*Cops*) and 24-hour cable (*Court TV*).

Chapter 3, 'The Criminal I: Erotic Thrillers, Neo-Noir and Trial Films', examines the re-emergence of neo-noir in the 1980s, and the new forms of criminality shown in the erotic thriller, offering familiar criminals (the gangster, the femme fatale) and new ones (the homme fatal). We take a closer look at three seminal films (*Body Heat*, *Fatal Attraction* (1987), *Basic Instinct* (1992)), along with another new crime cycle, the courtroom drama.

Chapter 4, 'The Criminal II: The Serial Killer Film and Postmodern Hybrids', closely examines two influential films of another new crime cycle: the serial killer film and *The Silence of the Lambs* and *Se7en*. We then turn to more recent crime films and the postmodern techniques of two contemporary auteurs, Quentin Tarantino (*Reservoir Dogs* (1992), *Pulp Fiction*), and David Lynch (*Blue Velvet* (1986), *Lost Highway* (1997), *Mulholland Dr.* (2001), *Inland Empire* (2006)). Where Lynch's films foreground the dreamlike (and frequently criminal) undercurrents of normality, Tarantino's films are self-reflexive homages to pop culture and cinematic history, which recreate many forms of the classic crime film, from the gangster to the heist and revenge film.

1   CRIME AS PUZZLE: WHODUNITS AND HEISTS

We start *in medias res*. It is night. A crowd of upper-class British suspects has been assembled in a room where a detective is about to reveal 'the identity of Lord Fenley's murderer', when at this dramatic moment, the film breaks down. It turns out we are watching *Murder at Midnight*, a film within the film *The Mirror Crack'd* (1980), being projected in the parish hall for Miss Marple and the other villagers of St Mary Mead. Fortunately for the frustrated villagers ('Oh dear, now we'll never know who did it'), Miss Marple runs through all the suspects, their motives and the relevant clues, and finally tells us that the murderer was 'Young Miss Kate'. Doubtful, one of the villagers says, 'She could be wrong, you know', to which another replies, 'She's not, I've seen the picture.'

Opening with this parody of the murder mystery made famous by Agatha Christie's crime fiction and cinematic adaptations like *And Then There Were None* (1945) and *Murder on the Orient Express* (1974), this sequence caricatures its classic elements: the dénouement scene in which the detective assembles all of the suspects of a recent crime (usually murder), announces the motives of each suspect, discusses all the clues and red herrings, shows logical reasoning in explaining hypotheses, inferences and deductions about the crime, and finally, dramatically reveals the identity of the real murderer. Like many adaptations of Christie's work in the 1970s, *The Mirror Crack'd* is a self-reflexive homage to the classic whodunit film of the 1940s, and an affectionate parody of the generic conventions of these crime stories. Why do murder mysteries continue to have such fascination for us? And why has the cinema repeatedly adapted the works of Arthur

Conan Doyle and Agatha Christie, amongst many others? As Miss Marple says: 'Human nature: the world of the cinema and the village. It's all the same really.' In the next three sections we shall take a look at three different types of crime text, in which the crime is presented as a narrative puzzle: the whodunit or classic mystery film, the television drama *CSI* and the heist film.

Classical form of the whodunit

'Murder is like a jigsaw. Until you fit in the final piece, you can't see the whole picture.'
— Miss Marple in *The Mirror Crack'd*

Epitomised by the classic characters created by Conan Doyle, Chesterton and Christie, and emerging out of the nineteenth-century development of the detective stories of Edgar Allan Poe and Eugène Sue, the classical 'whodunit' was long a staple of American and British cinema, reaching its highpoint in the 1930s with cycles of Sherlock Holmes, Philo Vance, Thin Man, Charlie Chan and the Mr Moto films and series. Similarly, first appearing in features of the 1930s and 1940s, Agatha Christie's classic detectives Hercule Poirot and Miss Marple returned in a cycle of 1970s films, and remain a staple of television to this day, influencing shows like *Murder She Wrote* (1984–96) and *Cadfael* (1994–98). The 'whodunit' refers to a classic murder mystery in which a detective, usually an amateur, must solve a crime that has baffled the police. The whodunit is a densely-plotted narrative, which focuses on the psychology of the suspects and criminals, the details of evidence and clues, the location of the crime scene, and the personal observations and eccentricities of detectives like the fussy and somewhat vain Belgian detective Hercule Poirot. Another variant of the crime investigator, the hard-boiled detective, will be a specific focus of chapter two, but in this chapter we will look in more detail at the whodunit and its investigation by the amateur sleuth.

Like the board game *Cluedo*™ (known as *Clue*™ in the US), which is also modelled on the formula of the whodunit (Colonel Mustard in the drawing room with a candlestick), the working out of the solution to the crime is a key pleasure in watching (and reading) mystery stories. Like the detective, we are concerned with a series of fundamental questions: who did it?

(identity of the murderer); why? (motive); when and where? (time and space are key issues); and finally, how? (the means). Some of these elements may be known at the beginning of the story; for example, the time and location of death may be calculated from the condition of the body, but all other questions must be considered and answered by the detective. Not unlike a crossword puzzle, whodunit narratives present complex factual scenarios, which both the viewer and detective decode, filling in the gaps. The story of the investigation suggests that the crime story is a problem of *knowledge*, which uses narrative devices of delay, obfuscation and fragmentation. In contrast to the thriller, the classic detective narrative is centripetal. Like a maze everything is tightly connected to the final solution of the narrative enigma, whereas the thriller has a looser, more centrifugal approach, with narrative digressions (Rubin 1999: 25). The whodunit moves backwards from effects to causes, whereas the thriller is the opposite, moving from causes to their effects, such as the outcome of a robbery in the heist film. Whereas the whodunit conceals the identity of the murderer, creating mystery, the thriller usually reveals this immediately, and whereas the whodunit focuses on the importance of what happened in the past, the thriller emphasises what will happen next, creating suspense (Todorov 1977: 44–5). Finally, the method of crime in the whodunit is usually exotic (with strange weapons or obscure poisons), whereas the thriller's method is straightforward (shooting or strangling) (Rubin 1999: 21–31).

In 'Aristotle on Detective Fiction' (first published in 1946), renowned mystery writer Dorothy L. Sayers described detective fiction as the 'art of framing lies', observing 'there is your recipe for detective fiction – make the readers believe the guilty innocent and the innocent guilty' (1980: 31). Unlike the hard-boiled detective, who may blur the social or class boundaries between the legal and criminal worlds, the amateur detective is morally impeccable, and restores social order by assigning guilt and innocence. The detective is also like a psychoanalyst, in that s/he begins with effects (clues/symptoms) and work backwards to figure out their origins. Like the emerging disciplines of criminology, psychiatry and the sciences in the nineteenth century, detective work privileged small, seemingly inconsequential details, and above all, celebrated knowledge, science, rationality and reasoning. For example, in *Mr Moto's Gamble* (1938), the Japanese super sleuth demonstrates the importance of scientific experiments to test hypotheses. In order to test whether poison on a boxing glove was splashed

on or smeared on, Moto says to his audience 'let us perform a little experiment using white ink to represent the poison'. Comparing the glove with
the photo of the murder victim's glove, he infers that the poison was in fact
splashed on, concluding 'class dismissed!' Here, like Moto's diegetic audience, the viewer becomes an eager pupil watching the demonstration of
Moto's deductive skills. *CSI: Crime Scene Investigation* continues this tradition today, offering the audience the thrill of looking at the evidence, posing
questions, suggesting hypotheses and making deductions from evidence.

The classic whodunit follows this typical pattern: either the amateur
detective is called to the scene of a crime, or more often is an accidental
witness, bystander or tourist, as when Hercule Poirot takes a holiday cruise
in *Death on the Nile* (1978), or stays on a resort island in Yugoslavia in *Evil
Under the Sun* (1981). The amateur detective is usually presented with some
version of a baffling crime (such as theft, or a murder), which takes place in
the classic scenario of a locked room (where a dead body is found, with no
apparent way for the murderer to enter and exit). In order to have a limited
cast of suspects, the narrative setting and/or the scene of the crime must
be restricted to, for example, a locked room (*Murders in the Rue Morgue*),
isolated country house (*And Then There Were None*), train (*Murder on the
Orient Express*), ship (*Death on the Nile*) or island (*Evil Under the Sun*). In
cinema, the confined space of the moving train, in which characters mys-
teriously vanish and bodies turn up in locked compartments, was repeatedly used in such films as Alfred Hitchcock's *The Lady Vanishes* (1939), Phil
Karlson's *The Shanghai Cobra* (1945) and Sidney Lumet's *Murder on the
Orient Express*. Consequently, space is always crucial to the crime story,
for, as Miss Marple says in *The Mirror Crack'd*, 'This is the spot where it
happened; which makes it so much easier to understand.' As part of the
revelation or interpretation of the crime, elaborate drawings, maps, blue-
prints or other visual material may be created or consulted by the detective,
which, together with the ways in which the *mise-en-scène* is framed and
photographed, enable the viewer to visualise the spatial dynamics of the
crime scene.

Simple objects like locks of hair, discarded cigarette butts or items
of personal jewellery are often important clues, and so the whodunit's
investigative process is often predicated on a fascination with *minutiae*.
This tradition continues in the importance of trace evidence in *CSI* like
skin cells, hair, blood or other potential evidence that can be examined

and linked back to a particular suspect. The detective's pursuit of clues leads to hypotheses about motive and means, and must be periodically re-evaluated in the light of new evidence. Clues are presented which both distract the viewer with *red herrings* (or false clues which lead to erroneous interpretations) or which turn out to be real evidence. Thus, in the film *The Adventures of Sherlock Holmes* (1939), Professor Moriarty (George Zucco) attempts to throw Holmes (Basil Rathbone) off the trail of his real plot to steal the British crown jewels by creating a distraction through a false clue: a drawing of a man carrying an albatross around his neck. Understanding Holmes' psychology and desire for novelty, Moriarty knows full well that Holmes would be fascinated with the cryptic drawing.

The word detective is derived from the French 'de-tegere', meaning to 'uncover' or 'expose the secret of'. Because 'tegere' comes from the word for thatch, a detective is someone who, figuratively speaking, 'takes the roof off', or uncovers the secrets found within. An astute knowledge of cause and effect, and superior deductive abilities are central to the solution of the crime. As Sherlock Holmes says: 'Elementary my dear Watson!' – a line which, incidentally, Holmes only ever said in the movies, and not in the original Conan Doyle stories. Like the protagonist in Voltaire's *Zadig* (1747), the amateur detective has an uncanny ability to predict specific physical or psychological details about the identity of the murderer, based on small clues found at the crime scene. For example, in *The Adventures of Sherlock Holmes*, Holmes examines some footprints and deduces that the owner is club-footed, and from Bolivia or Chile! These character traits continue to influence contemporary crime drama on television, including professional detectives like Robert Goren (Vincent D'Onofrio) on *Law and Order: Criminal Intent* (2001–present). Together with Gil Grissom (William Petersen), the criminalist in the enormously popular TV series *CSI* (2000–present), amateur or professional detectives like Goren, Miss Marple, Sherlock Holmes and Poirot all share acute observational skills, psychological insight into behaviour and motivation, high intelligence (or what the Belgian detective Poirot calls his 'little grey cells') and an almost magical command of arcane knowledge, in addition to a fair share of eccentricities (for example, Poirot's penchant for hairnets and handcream, which mark him out as foreign in Christie's xenophobic terms). Furthermore, in the whodunit, the detective is usually an amateur or non-professional like Sherlock Holmes or Miss Marple, whose intellectual abilities rather than professional training lead to their continuous involvement in the solving of crime (although Poirot, as a former Belgian police officer, is one exception to this rule. Nonetheless, as his service was brief, and his work is carried out as a retiree, he can be considered an amateur). As Sherlock Holmes declares in *The Adventures of Sherlock Holmes*, 'I interfere wherever and whenever I like.'

Figures like the obtuse Inspector Lestrade serve to highlight the superior intellect and investigative skills of Sherlock Holmes, and these hapless figures inevitably end up handing over the case to the amateur detective, whose worldwide fame as incomparable sleuths has already been established as longstanding. In the course of the investigation the detective offers sage or witty observations, as with the pseudo-Confucianisms of Charlie Chan: 'Murder like potato chips – cannot stop at just one.' The detective interviews all the suspects, and reveals that most of them have a direct or indirect motive to kill (usually for greed or passion or revenge), and then presents the solution to the crime, in a room where all the suspects are assembled. Sometimes the crime itself is re-enacted through flashbacks, narrated by the detective. As part of the revelation of the crime, characters often turn out to have secret identities or pasts, which may in turn provide motives to kill. Thus, in *Murder on the Orient Express*, all twelve suspects turn out to have a prior personal or professional relationship to the murder victim, Mr Ratchett (Richard Widmark), whose real identity as the mobster Cassetti, together with his involvement in the kidnapping and murder of little Daisy Armstrong (a thinly-veiled version of the Lindbergh baby kidnapping), turns out to be the key motivation for the crime (which all twelve suspects jointly committed). In this final encounter of detective and suspects, the dénouement and revelation of the real killer (and motive) is thus highly *theatricalised*, recalling the literary origins of the crime film.

Sherlock Holmes has been one of the most popular detectives of all time, appearing on television and film in over 250 movies, and hundreds of radio and stage plays, from the silent era to the present day. First introduced by Arthur Conan Doyle in his novel *A Study in Scarlet* (1887), he was described by the narrator in 'A Scandal in Bohemia' as 'the most perfect reasoning and observing machine that the world has seen'. This violin-playing social recluse and cocaine addict was the subject of sixty stories and four novels published between 1887 and 1927. In 1893, in 'The Final Problem', Conan Doyle killed off Sherlock Holmes and his nemesis Professor Moriarty in a spectacular plummet over the Reichenbach Falls. So extensive

Fig. 4 The most 'perfect reasoning and observing machine': Basil Rathbone as Sherlock Holmes

was the outcry over Holmes' death (people even began wearing mourning armbands on the streets of London), Conan Doyle was forced to bring his detective back to life in *The Hound of the Baskervilles* (published serially in 1901–1902), and again in 'The Adventure of the Empty House' (1903), with a novel (*The Valley of Fear*) and several more collections of Sherlock Holmes stories published before Conan Doyle's death in 1930.

Some of the best entries in the extensive Holmes visual canon include 14 films starring Basil Rathbone as Holmes and Nigel Bruce as Dr Watson, beginning with *The Adventures of Sherlock Holmes* and *The Hound of the Baskervilles* in 1939 and concluding with *Dressed to Kill* in 1946. (In *Crazy House* (1943) Rathbone only makes a cameo appearance.) Holmes has been played by more than 88 actors, including Peter Cushing, John Barrymore, Christopher Lee, Clive Brook and Christopher Plummer (see Robertson 2001: 51). He has been the subject of British, German, Danish and American silent film versions, from the first Holmes adaptation *Sherlock Holmes Baffled* (1900–03), to animated films (*The Great Mouse Detective* (1986)), children's television (*The Young Sherlock Holmes* (1985)), and in parodies like Buster Keaton's *Sherlock Jr.* (1924) and Gene Wilder's *Adventure of Sherlock Holmes' Smarter Brother* (1975), amongst many other comedies. *The Hound of the Baskervilles* was most frequently adapted to film, from the German silent series *Der Hund von Baskervilles* (1914–20) to Hammer Pictures' colour production in 1958, as well as in numerous television series from Britain, Canada and the United States over the last hundred years. Although we often associate Sherlock Holmes with late Victorian London, which the Conan Doyle stories recreated in such fascinating detail, many of the earliest films had contemporary settings, including the 1920s' two-reelers from British company Stoll, and the five films of the 1930s, which starred Arthur Wontner as Holmes (beginning with *The Sleeping Cardinal/Sherlock Holmes' Fatal Hour* in 1931). Similarly, the twelve films that Rathbone and Bruce made for Universal Studios between 1942 and 1946 had contemporary settings, thus obviating the need for expensive period sets, and enabling the integration of war-related spy stories into the narrative.

Although we commonly assume that he uses the process of deduction, Holmes in fact uses *induction*, a process of intellectual reasoning that infers a generalised conclusion from a particular instance. For example, in *The Hound of the Baskervilles* (1958) Holmes (Peter Cushing) uses induction to describe the identity, behaviour and character of a person, based on a personal item of clothing. The mystery of Dr Mortimer's walking stick, which is left behind one day, becomes a pretext for both Watson and Holmes to describe its owner, sight unseen. Dr Watson examines the stick, and suggests that the owner is an old country doctor and a member of a hunt club, but Holmes demurs, suggesting instead that he is 'amiable, unambitious, under thirty and in possession of a dog'. He infers these conclusions by observing that an inscription on the stick 'CCH', stands for Charing Cross Hospital; that the doctor was given the walking stick as a gift by his former colleagues before he moved to the country (and thus he is unambitious, abandoning a London medical career); that he is forgetful (because he has left his stick); and finally, a dog owner (because the stick is covered in canine bite marks). Holmes' hypotheses are all confirmed when Mortimer later turns up to reclaim his stick. Mortimer also becomes a narrative pretext for Conan Doyle to allude to current theories of criminality; Mortimer wants to measure Holmes' skull (phrenology), discusses Cesare Lombroso's theories of criminal atavism, and also refers to Alphonse Bertillon as the 'number one man of science'. Similarly, in *The Sign of Four* (1983) Holmes examines a watch and observes that the owner is 'a man of untidy habits who lived for some time in poverty, with occasional short intervals of prosperity, but finally taking to drink, died'. Holmes infers the owner's careless and untidy nature because the watch is full of dents from being thoughtlessly placed in a pocket full of loose change; that he was in intermittent poverty from the four pawn numbers scratched on the watch; and that he is an alcoholic from the grooves found on the keyhole for winding the watch which was 'evidence of an unsteady hand'. Dr Watson is stunned to discover a perfect description of his brother, who is the owner of the watch. As Holmes' assistant, Watson acts as a foil, and through his false hypotheses illustrates the detective's superior reasoning. Similarly, in *Evil Under the Sun*, the owner of the resort hotel, Daphne (Maggie Smith), is a comic foil to Poirot (Peter Ustinov), offering theories, equal parts bizarre and absurd ('cherchez la femme', and 'cherchez la fruit!') about who has killed Arlena Stewart (Diana Rigg), and backing up her theories by telling of a child murderer (in 'Hungary – or was it Crete'), who used a pair of nutcrackers to strangle someone.

Whereas the hard-boiled detective story and crime thrillers of the 1940s concentrated on the social milieu of the criminal, the British whodunit was often centrally concerned with class, featuring aristocratic locations and characters. Because the whodunit was written largely by British authors (Christie, Conan Doyle, Chesterton), it also featured exotic locales, such as the mysterious Dartmoor (*Hound of the Baskervilles*), or colonial settings. Watson has served in India as he reminds us in films like *Terror by Night* (1946), and whodunits often linked colonial locations like Palestine, India or the African continent with valuable jewels or *objets d'art*, which become the 'MacGuffiin' (a term used by Alfred Hitchcock in 1939 to describe a plot device that advances the story or provides character motivation, but otherwise does not have much relevance in the film) or narrative pretext for the crime, as with the Star of Rhodesia in *Terror by Night*, the Star of Delhi – 'the largest emerald in the world' – in *The Adventures of Sherlock Holmes*, or The Great Moghul, the 'second largest diamond in the world' in *The Sign of Four*.

Reflecting its sensational literary origins, the whodunit's exoticism was often linked to the supernatural or socially fantastic. In 1930s' and 1940s' crime films, this frequently took the form of orientalism or a narrative fascination with Asian characters or settings, usually presented in stereotyped form. Charlie Chan and Mr Moto as, respectively, Chinese and Japanese detectives continued this Orientalist tradition, in which stories were set in Chinatown, or featured exotic murder weapons like the Cobra in *The Shanghai Cobra*, which killed its victims by puncturing them with deadly cobra venom. Warner Oland starred in 18 Chan pictures, and on his death was replaced by Sidney Toler (11 pictures for Fox from 1938–42), and in turn by Roland Winters – in all cases, non-Asian actors. Similarly, Moto was played by Hungarian-born Peter Lorre. The eight *Mr Moto* films were based on John P. Marquand's *Saturday Evening Post* serial, which began with 'Mr Moto Takes a Hand' in 1935, and Moto's first film appearance was in *Think Fast Mr Moto* (1937). The series of Moto pictures ran for two years between 1937 and 1939, ending when World War Two made the Japanese hero detective politically untenable. Like the Sherlock Holmes, Agatha Christie and Charlie Chan films, the Moto series featured exotic locations, from Puerto Rico to Angkor Wat and Port Said; exotic 'MacGuffins', like the Queen of Sheba's crown; or bizarre criminals, such as Metaxa in *Mr Moto Takes a Vacation* (1939). But the most exotic villain of them all, the dastardly Fu Manchu, would return repeatedly in films, television and radio series, matching wits with his nemesis, Sir Dennis Nayland Smith of Scotland Yard, in the British serial *The Mystery of Dr Fu-Manchu* (1923) and the American feature *The Mysterious Dr Fu Manchu* (1929). Based on the Sax Rohmer (pseudonym for Arthur Henry Ward) character that first appeared in *The Story-teller* in 1912, he initially appeared in prototype form as Mr King in *The Yellow Claw* (1920) and unofficially in the earlier *The Mysterious Wu Chung Foo* (1914), but would be most famously played by Boris Karloff in *The Mask of Fu Manchu* (1932).

With *Murder on the Orient Express*, not only did glamorous and exotic *mise-en-scène* function as narrative spectacle in the whodunit, but like the spy thrillers of the 1940s, travel, border-crossing and wealthy tourism were prominent in the narrative. An international group of tourists on a cruise up the Nile (*Death on the Nile*), or on holiday at a resort island in the Adriatic (*Death Under the Sun*), or on a boat trip from Trieste to Jaffa, with a side visit to an archaeological dig in the Holy Land (*Appointment With Death* (1988)), are all examples of the ways in which glamorous upper-class tourism in the interwar years became a narrative setting for crime. In addition it provided a justification for the international cast, frequently used in films of the 1970s, from the disaster movie (*Poseidon Adventure* (1972), *Towering Inferno* (1974), *Airport '75* (1974)) to drama (*Hotel* (1967)), and which emphasised glamorous locations and casting over plot. The Christie whodunit was usually an international co-production featuring star ensembles (Ingrid Bergman, Diana Rigg, James Mason, Richard Widmark, Anthony Perkins) playing national stereotypes, from the brash American (Lauren Bacall) to the effete or eccentric Englishman (John Gielgud), or dotty Englishwoman (Maggie Smith). The popularity of the Christie murder mystery continues, largely in television series, to this day (*Agatha Christie's Marple*, starring Joan Hickson, 1984–92 and Geraldine McEwan, 2004–present; *Agatha Christie's Poirot*, starring David Suchet, 1989–93, 1995, two television specials, series resumes, 1996–present). An anime television series called *Agatha Christie's Great Detectives Poirot and Marple* (2004–5) brought the two famous detectives together in one series with adaptations of many of Christie's most famous stories.

Agatha Christie's spinster detective Jane Marple has appeared on film, television and radio and been most notably performed by Helen Hayes, Angela Lansbury, Margaret Rutherford, Joan Hickson and Geraldine McEwan. Miss Marple hails from the village of St Mary Mead and like the detective played by Peter Falk in the later television series *Columbo* (1971–1993, intermittently), hides astute intelligence and razor-sharp observational skills beneath the deceptive surface of, in this instance, a little old lady, who is described by the Scotland Yard Inspector she consistently trumps in detective skills, as 'a grey-haired cobra [who] sticks to this business like chewing gum to a cat' (*Murder at the Vicarage*, 1986). The incongruous spinster in a little English village in the countryside who, notwithstanding her sheltered existence, solves crimes by her astute insight into human nature was, according to Christie, modelled on her own grandmother, who 'always expected the worst of everyone and everything and was, with almost frightening accuracy, usually proved right' (quoted in Stasio 2005: B21). Both Columbo and Miss Marple utilise humour arising from their apparently timorous personas.

The whodunit also often included comedic elements through minor characters like the detective's assistant. In the American Charlie Chan serials, for example, Chan's 'number one son' and his chauffeur Birmingham (frequently played by Mantan Moreland) provided comic relief in the form of racial stereotypes as they helped investigate the crime. Comedy was a strong element in the escapades of Nick (William Powell) and Nora (Myrna Loy) Charles, a pair of affluent New York dipsomaniacal detectives. Blending the detective story with the screwball comedies then popular in the 1930s (*Twentieth Century* (1934), *Bringing Up Baby* (1938)), Dashiell Hammett's *The Thin Man* (1934) spawned five sequels. Like Sherlock Holmes before him, Nick Charles always staged the classic confrontation scene with all the suspects, as he does in *Shadow of the Thin Man* (1941), observing that 'one thing about a murder case, if you just let people talk long enough, sooner or later somebody spills the beans'. Coincidentally, William Powell began his career with a small role in *Sherlock Holmes* (1922), and also played Philo Vance in another series of detective films including *The Kennel Murder Case* (1933).

Remembering that the whodunit is an exercise in competing narratives between the detective and the various suspects, it often featured a surprising degree of self-reflexivity, long before the self-consciousness of postwar cinema. Todd Berliner describes this as a 'genre breaker' or a film that 'loudly broadcasts its violation of tradition, inviting audiences to join in the film's efforts to expose, and often mock, genre conventions', and exemplified by self-reflexive whodunits like *The Last of Sheila* (1973), *Murder by Death* (1976) or *Clue* (1985) (2001: 25). In the dénouement scene in *Evil Under the Sun*, when he is confronted by Poirot as the murderer, Patrick Redfern (Nicholas Clay) acerbically reviews Poirot's performance, as if it were a play, wryly remarking 'excellent plot line, imaginatively conceived, good clear narrative style, I'll give you nine out of ten'. In *The Mirror Crack'd* self-reflexivity abounds: from the film within the film, to Elizabeth Taylor and Kim Novak playing divas not unlike themselves, to visual allusions to *Suspicion* (the poisoned spoon), and to a Scotland Yard Inspector Dermot

Craddock (Edward Fox) who is a film fan, *The Mirror Crack'd* invites spectators to recognise and enjoy its play with the history and conventions of the whodunit.

CSI: Crime Scene Investigation

The enormously popular television series *CSI: Crime Scene Investigation* and its two spin-offs *CSI Miami* (2002–present) and *CSI New York* (2004–present) are not a new concept in television as popular forensic dramas like *The Expert* (1968–71, 1976), *Quincy M.E.* (1976–83), *State Coroner* (1997–98) and *Da Vinci's Inquest* (1998–2005) have demonstrated. These series share important parallels with the classic whodunit because the primary emphasis of the show is on solving the puzzle by scientific deduction and the interpretation of evidence. Forensic dramas are also a form of the police procedural, in that they focus on the everyday work of crime investigators. Like the classic whodunit, *CSI*'s lead forensic specialist Gil Grissom, together with his team, emphasises the importance that erudition, specialised knowledge and training play in the solution of crime. But unlike the mundane investigative work of police procedurals like *Dragnet*, *CSI* glamorises and expands the professional role of the criminalists whose primary function is the collection and analysis of physical evidence at a crime scene. This is particularly evident on *CSI Miami*, which turns its criminalists into police officers who carry guns, and interrogate and arrest suspects.

Like the whodunit, *CSI* emphasises the importance of deductive and inductive reasoning, interpretation and hypothesis. Its creators understand the solution to a crime as encoded within the trace evidence which remains behind, cast off by the criminal, victim or weapon; as the criminalists repeatedly remind us in the show's mantras: 'the evidence will tell us' and the 'evidence speaks for the victims'. There are three major types of identification: archival identification, which links the criminal body to itself across space and time (such as a mug shot); diagnostic identification, which reads signs of potential criminality in the body (such as forensic psychology); and forensic identification, which links a specific criminal act to a specific criminal body (such as a murderer leaving a fingerprint at the crime). Solving the mystery is the objective in the classic whodunit and *CSI* foregrounds the role which technology plays in the investigation of crime, through visual *revela-*

tion. One of the defining characteristics of the show is its visual spectacle which, through special effects and make-up, show unusual or conventionally impossible camera angles, such as the impact of a bullet on a chest, or the constriction of the throat when a character is strangled or drowns. With the aid of snorkel cameras, or tiny cameras on snake-like appendages that can move through very small spaces, the camera flies through artificial mock-ups of the human body, showing it from the inside out, and thereby making visual spectacle educational. These spectacular sequences are usually accompanied by voice-overs that comment on and describe what we are seeing, continuing the whodunit tradition of revelation. Through other techniques such as fuming superglue, fingerprints come to light on irregular surfaces like plastic bags; and through tests with reagents, infrared cameras and special glasses, bodily substances such as blood, semen or other fluids light up. With the aid of special chemicals or machines such as electron microscopes (often used to check for gunshot residue), gas chromotographs (which separate the elements of compounds) and mass spectrometers (which separate and identify elements in compounds), trace evidence that would otherwise be undetectable become visible to the spectator or camera in privileged point-of-view shots or close-ups, and the show repeatedly emphasises the importance of the *microscopic*.

Like the amateur detective in the classical whodunit, *CSI* and its spin-offs combine a primary focus on the detection of crime with characters with back-stories and personal quirks. The CSI team includes the alcoholic Sara Sidle (Jorja Fox); a gambler, Warwick Brown (Gary Dourdan); the cocky Nick Stokes (George Eads); a single-mother and former Vegas stripper Catherine Willows (Marg Helgenberger); the socially inept Greg Sanders (Eric Szmanda); and a gruff detective, Brass (Paul Guilfoyle). Heading up the team is the idiosyncratic Grissom, a shy loner, who is losing his hearing (and was raised by a deaf mother). Like Holmes and Poirot, Grissom is often ready with a literary allusion, which usually occurs in the show's prologue, before the opening credits. In the episode 'Got Murder?' (Season 3, 2003), when confronted with an eyeball that a raven has brought back to its nest, the team must figure out how to find the body that belongs to the eyeball. As usual, Grissom begins the show with a literary allusion, this time to Poe: 'quoth the raven, never more, never more'. Grissom has a particular fascination for insects; and as a forensic entomologist, or expert in the life cycles and habits of insects, his specialist training is used to estimate the time of death of the victim, based on the age of insects found on the corpse or at the crime scene. Other such specialties featured on the show include forensic anthropology (which reconstructs the facial appearance of victims, from the bone structure of their skulls); ballistics (the analysis of weaponry and bullets); forensic psychiatry (the creation and analysis of psychological profiles of suspects); and forensic odontology (the analysis of dental evidence such as bite wounds and the identification of remains based on dental records). All these specialist sub-fields offer what is a key dimension of the show – the spectacle of *seeing* something which is either hidden (because it is microscopic in scale) or otherwise undetectable without special tests and equipment. The show also creates pleasure through pedagogy: dialogue is shaped to educate the audience about the specialist training and technology used to interpret a crime scene, focusing on fascinating details such as the particular shape that glass assumes when it is broken from the inside out (as opposed to the outside in), the particular pattern that blood drops form (depending on whether they are dripped, smeared or splattered), and so on. Educational aspects also include editing patterns that show us the point of view of the criminalists as they look through their microscopes or analyse their chemical printouts, thereby inviting us to share in the pleasure of interpretation and deduction. *CSI* represents science and technology as sexy, and has led to increased enrolments in forensic training programmes across the US. Whereas the forensic drama like the whodunit offers the viewer the pleasure of interpreting the crime scene evidence in order to reconstruct the crime, in the next section we look at another type of crime story, in which spectatorial pleasure is in watching the execution of a difficult crime.

The heist film

The heist, or caper, film is a cycle or sub-genre of crime films that feature an elaborately planned and executed robbery, and whose narratives emphasise the logistical and technical difficulties of a crime and its execution. In the postwar period, a number of film noir, gangster and crime films placed greater narrative emphasis on the logistical aspects of a crime, as we see with the robbery of a train and a raid on a chemical plant in the James Cagney gangster film *White Heat* (1949). With roots in American film noir (*The Killing, Criss Cross* (1949)), and French noir (*Du Rififi chez les hommes* (1955), *Bob le Flambeur* (1955)), the heist film began with *The Asphalt Jungle* in 1950 and early examples include *Armored Car Robbery* (1950), *The Big Caper* (1957), *Ocean's Eleven* (1960), *Topkapi* (1964), *How to Steal a Million* (1966), *The Thomas Crown Affair* (1968) and *The Italian Job* (1969). The classic heist film has a three-act structure: the first act staking out and observing the robbery site; the second, the execution of the crime; and the third, the (usually unsuccessful) aftermath of the crime. The narrative emphasises the importance of planning, preparation and timing, and the smooth teamwork necessary to carry out a difficult heist. The heist film offers the spectator the pleasure of the conceptual challenge which faces the robbers in the logistical planning and execution of the crime, the thrills of the crime's successful execution, and even a vicarious delight in the team double-crossing each other after their initial success. For example, Jules Dassin's *Du Rififi chez les hommes* is a story about a jewellery heist in Paris. Based on a story by crime writer Auguste Le Breton, it featured a famous 25-minute dialogue-free sequence showing a break-in, including the use of a fire extinguisher to silence a vibration-sensitive alarm system. Starring Jean Servais as Tony le Stéphanois, who leads the crew of robbers, *Rififi*, together with *Touchez pas au Grisbi* (*Honour Among Thieves* (1954)), triggered a cinematic French crime wave that built on the earlier French tradition of the *policier*.

The heist film has certain parallels with war films like *The Dirty Dozen* (1967) and *Kelly's Heroes* (1970), which featured a team of men tasked with carrying out a difficult, suicidal mission, and with later television shows such as *Mission: Impossible* (1966–73). Time is always of the essence: the time of security patrols, the time when alarms switch on and off, the limited time after the break-in before the police arrive, and so on. Thus, in *Heat* (1995) there are exactly three minutes to carry out the armoured car robbery, before the police arrive. Watches must be synchronised, and plans must be meticulous. In keeping with the thematic importance of time is the significant role that chance and fate play in these stories. The thieves often talk about what they plan to do with the money after they steal it (*The Getaway* (1972 and 1994), *Set It Off* (1996), *The Heist* (1999)), thus accentuating the importance of the future, and what the money emotionally represents to the robbers. In *The Asphalt Jungle* Dix Handley (Sterling Hayden) says: 'First thing I'm going to do is take a bath in the creek and get this city dirt off me.' He plans to buy back the family farm and horses which his father lost when he was a child. Led by Dix and Doc Erwin Riedenschneider (Sam Jaffe) the team plans a heist of a jewellery store worth $500,000. Doc comes up with the plan while he is in jail for a 'caper he did so long ago, I'd forgotten about it', and when he is released, he goes about hiring members of his crew, including the specialist 'boxman' (safecracker), driver and 'hooligan' (or muscle). As the master planner Doc wryly observes, after everything has gone wrong in the robbery: '[We] put in hours and hours of planning everything down to the last detail. Burglar alarms start going off all over for no sensible reason. Then what? A gun fires of its own accord and a man is shot. And a broken down *harness* [cop], no good for anything but chasing kids has to trip over us. Blind accident. What can you do against blind accident?'

Like *The Asphalt Jungle*, *The Killing* has a quasi-documentary feel, with a complex and chronologically-overlapping narrative structure, which is broken down into segments that focus on each member of the team, accompanied by voice-overs like '...at seven am'. Johnny Clay (Sterling Hayden) has just been released from a five-year prison sentence, and plans a racetrack heist. Many heists depend upon diversions which distract witnesses and security guards while the actual robbery occurs. In *The Killing* there are two: the shooting of a racehorse, and the eruption of a bar fight at the track. For both of these tasks, subcontractors are hired for a specific fee, rather than a cut of the ultimate proceeds. Like *Rififi* the robbery, which initially is successful, ultimately fails. The heist team consists of three men, each of whom is paired up with a romantic interest. George and Sherry Peatty (Elisha Cook Jr and Marie Windsor) are the couple whose actions lead to the failure and death of most of the team. Sherry is secretly cheating on her husband with another man, who finds out about the robbery, and wants to double-cross the team. After various killings, only Johnny is left alive to flee with his girlfriend Fay (Coleen Gray) and the money. He is forced to check his suitcase containing the money into an airplane's cargo, but the suitcase falls off the luggage handler's trolley and breaks open, and the money blows all over the tarmac. Similarly, in *Rififi*, one member of the gang gets greedy and steals extra jewels, which he gives to his girlfriend, and as a result, despite the successful outcome of the robbery, a rival gang finds out about the haul and tries to rob them in turn, and everyone ends up dead. By the 1960s, and unlike the fatalism of the earlier heist films of French and American noir, the crooks usually get away with the crime (*Charley Varrick*),

Fig. 5 Comedic cool: the heist crew of *Ocean's Eleven* (2001)

although sometimes the heist would end with an ironic twist, as when the original *Ocean's Eleven* ends with the money accidentally burnt. Despite a number of double-crosses in *The Getaway*, Doc McCoy (Steve McQueen) and Carol (Ali McGraw) manage to escape with $500,000 from a bank robbery, after hiding out in a garbage truck that dumps them at the city tip. Adapted from a Jim Thompson novel, *The Getaway* would later be remade by Roger Donaldson in 1994 with another on- and off-screen couple – Alec Baldwin and Kim Basinger.

The heist narrative emphasised the logistical planning and training of the criminal group, many of whom had individual specialist skills and the rounding-up of the team according to these skills has become one of the key conventions of the heist movie. In Steven Soderbergh's remake, *Ocean's Eleven* (2001), the formation of the gang, and their practising of the crime, are key aspects of the plot, with characters such as Basher Tarr (Don Cheadle) the computer specialist, or Linus Caldwell (Matt Damon) the gifted pickpocket, being sourced by the gang leaders played by Brad Pitt and George Clooney. Here the team members buy a replica safe and practise on it, and at the same time, shoot a fake image of the safe that will later be plugged into the casino's video surveillance. Midway through the story, the group has achieved social and professional cohesion and is ready for the execution of the robbery itself, which usually presents at least one unexpected hitch, before the successful outcome of the crime.

In the 1950s and 1960s the British heist film often took a comedic turn, as with *The Italian Job*, in which a team played by Michael Caine, Noel Coward and Benny Hill, amongst others, execute a complicated plan to steal $4 million in gold bars in Rome by setting up an elaborate traffic jam, as they make their getaway in minis driving down into the subway. Led by Charley Croker (Caine), a harsh taskmaster, the film emphasises the gang's comedic incompetence rather than slick teamwork, and the film ends with the team's gold bars about to fall off a bus suspended over an alpine cliff. Sometimes the heist was combined with romantic comedy, as in *Topkapi*, in which Peter Ustinov, in an Academy Award-winning performance, leads a team of robbers to steal a fabulous jewelled Ottoman dagger from the Topkapi museum in Istanbul. Unlike the American heist film, most British heist films emphasise the events before or after the robbery, and focus on the gang's interpersonal conflicts. Quentin Tarantino's *Reservoir Dogs* was an example of the revival of the American heist film, but following the British narrative model. The heist film has made a comeback in recent years with many remakes, that in some ways are improvements on the originals, with *Ocean's Eleven* and *The Italian Job* (2003) as two notable examples. Like his other crime films (such as *Collateral*) and TV series (*Miami Vice*, *Crime Story*, *Robbery Homicide*), Michael Mann's *Heat* is a visual meditation on the city of Los Angeles, with striking cinematography and unusual locations. It is a psychological study of robber Neil McCauley (Robert De Niro), who with Chris Shiherlis (Val Kilmer) plans an armoured car robbery in LA while matching wits with Detective Vincent Hanna (Al Pacino). Mann parallels the professional and personal lives of cop and robber, who have failed or dysfunctional marriages, are emotional loners and who live only for their work. As Hanna's wife says to him: 'You don't live with me, you live among the remains of dead people.' Mann's film is an example of neo-noir (see chapter three) and thus its ending adopts the bleak pessimism of classic noir. Citing Peter Yates's *Bullitt* the final shoot-out scene at LA airport copies the similar scene between Frank Bullitt (Steve McQueen) and the Killer (John Aprea) at San Francisco's airport which in both films ends with the death of the criminal. However, unlike *Bullitt*, Mann's film shows the tragic yet intimate bond between cop and criminal, suggesting that ultimately they are emotional twins as dedicated professionals and loners. In the next chapter, we look more closely at some of these dedicated professionals who investigate crime: from the hard-boiled detective to the police officer and lawyer.

2   THE PROFESSIONAL CRIME SOLVER:
FROM HARD-BOILED DETECTIVES TO CRUSADING COPS

Hard-boiled detectives in film noir: 1941–58

> 'Whoever went to the movies with any regularity during 1946 was
> caught in the midst of Hollywood's profound postwar affection for
> morbid drama. From January through December deep shadows,
> clutching hands, exploding revolvers, sadistic villains and heroines
> tormented with deeply rooted diseases of the mind flashed across
> the screen in a panting display of psychoneuroses, unsublimated
> sex and murder most foul.'
> > – D. Marsham *Life* (25 August 1947)

What *Life* magazine described as a new kind of 'morbid drama' in 1947
(cited in Schatz 1981: 111) identified a type of postwar American film that
has come to be known as *film noir*. The term refers to dark or black film,
and was first used by Nino Frank in reference to four crime films: *The
Maltese Falcon* (1941), *Murder, My Sweet* (1944), *Double Indemnity* (1944)
and *Laura* (1944) in Paris in 1946. In this chapter we are going to take a
closer look at the professional criminal investigator, and we begin with
the hard-boiled detective who appeared in many film noirs, or a cycle of
crime films (many of them low-budget) made between the early 1940s and
the late 1950s. Film critics have vigorously debated whether film noir can
be considered a genre, a style or a historical cycle of films, but it is not a
label that the film industry used, which instead marketed these films as
crime stories, psychological thrillers, melodramas or suspense pictures.

Noir films shared similar visual styles, narrative strategies, characterisation and subject matter, and had their roots in German Expressionism, French Poetic Realism and American hard-boiled pulp fiction. Stylistically, noir films were characterised by chiaroscuro lighting (or dramatic contrasts of light and shadow), tight frames, oblique compositions, canted camera angles, long takes, deep focus, distorting wide-angle lenses and static camerawork. As a style, noir crossed several different genres, including the thriller, melodrama, gangster and detective films, and even influenced comedies, westerns and musicals. Its *mise-en-scène* featured urban night-life, rain-slicked streets, swanky nightclubs and deserted alleyways, and its narratives were characterised by complex chronologies, voice-overs, ellipses and flashbacks (Spicer 2002: 4). Like the hard-boiled detective novel that it frequently adapted, noir films were usually set in the urban spaces of New York, Los Angeles, Chicago or San Francisco. Through subjective flashbacks and voice-overs (and sometimes point-of-view camerawork in *Lady in the Lake* and *Dark Passage* (1947)), the spectator is anchored to the story through the perspective of the protagonist, whose knowledge may be as incomplete and partial as our own. In keeping with its dark visual style, noir was a profoundly pessimistic form with recurring themes of paranoia, dread, claustrophobia, fatalism and entrapment. Film noir encompassed several kinds of crime stories, including quasi-documentaries and police procedurals (*T-Men*, *The Naked City*, *Call Northside 777* (1948)); heist films (*The Killing*, *The Asphalt Jungle*); private eye stories (*The Big Sleep*, *Murder, My Sweet*); sexual love triangles with a femme fatale (*The Postman Always Rings Twice*, *Double Indemnity*, *Out of the Past* (1947)); and innocent bystander stories (*The Hitch-hiker*, *The Wrong Man* and *Detour* (1945)).

According to Foster Hirsch, film noir's basic narrative concerns have remained 'the private-investigation quest, crimes of passion and profit, stories involving masquerade, amnesia, split identity, and double and triple crosses' (1999: 14). Feminist film critics have focused on issues of gender, with a particular interest in the quasi-criminal figure of the *femme fatale* (literally 'fatal woman'). During World War Two women entered the workforce in large numbers and this important social development was indirectly reflected in film noir's anxieties about independent assertive women like the femme fatale, who through their powerful sexuality lure hapless male protagonists into crime and death.

Often an ex-police officer or ex-GI, noir protagonists were usually alienated, ambivalent and sometimes psychologically disturbed men; and as such noir suggested profound anxieties about masculinity. The cycle often dramatised the psychological illnesses and alienation of the returning war veteran like American Buzz Wanchek (William Bendix) in *The Blue Dahlia* or Englishman Clem Morgan (Trevor Howard) in *They Made Me a Fugitive* (1947), who failed to fit into postwar society because of their wartime experiences or injuries. Noir stories were also portraits of criminal sociopaths like Tommy Udo (Richard Widmark), the giggling sadist who pushes a woman in a wheelchair down a flight of stairs in *Kiss of Death*, or like Vince Stone (Lee Marvin), the cruel gangster who throws a cup of scalding coffee in his girlfriend's face in *The Big Heat* (1953).

In the 1930s, the hard-boiled detective emerged in a new form of popular, commercial and realist American fiction by Raymond Chandler, Dashiell Hammett, Cornell Woolrich and James M. Cain, whose work exemplified a new vernacular of colloquial dialogue, wisecracks and fractured syntax. Not only was this hard-boiled literature an Americanisation of the crime story, but as Frank Krutnik (1991) suggests, it was also a profoundly *masculine* crime story. In the classic hard-boiled novel of Chandler and Hammett, suspense, violence and menace were minimal, but with later writers like Jim Thompson and Mickey Spillane, the detective became a 'vehicle for brutal violence' (Lee 2003: 81). The hard-boiled detective story has its roots in the adventure stories of characters like Nick Carter (first created in 1886 by Ormond G. Smith and John Russell Coryell), and in pulp fiction magazines like *Speakeasy*, *Gun Molls Magazine*, *Mystery Stories* and *Gangster Stories*. The most famous of these magazines, *The Black Mask*, published stories by Chandler, Hammett and Erle Stanley Gardner. Chandler's Philip Marlowe (1939–58), Dashiell Hammett's Sam Spade (1930–44) and Mickey Spillane's Mike Hammer (1947–present) were the three major character series of the classic noir period. Spillane was the most commercially popular of all the hard-boiled writers, averaging 4 to 5 million copies in sales per novel, and until the mid-1960s seven of the top-30 best-selling books were written by him (see Inciardi & Dee 1987: 98). Meanwhile, Chandler's Marlowe appeared in four films in the 1940s, one in the 1960s and three in the 1970s, and was played by Humphrey Bogart, Dick Powell, George Montgomery, Robert Montgomery, James Garner, Elliot Gould and Robert Mitchum. In 1931 the detective story expanded into the comic strip, with the release of Chester

Gould's *Dick Tracy*, which was followed by *Detective Comics* in 1937. There were new American film series in the 1930s and 1940s centered on private eyes like Boston Blackie (1941–49) and Michael Shayne, the eponymous Irish detective played by Lloyd Nolan in seven films from 1940 to 1942, and there were also mysterious crime avengers like The Whistler and The Shadow, all of whom appeared in numerous feature films, adventure/mystery serials or radio series. Meanwhile in Britain, hard-boiled writers like John Creasey, James Curtis, Walter Greenwood and Peter Cheyney (with private eye Lemmy Caution) were influenced by their American counterparts, but other crime films like the fifty adaptations of Edgar Wallace's 'shocker' stories between 1925 and 1939 showed the continuing influence of the Gothic literary tradition (Spicer 2002: 178–9). Graham Greene's novels and screenplays blended both traditions in a series of both British and American cinematic adaptations (*The Third Man*, *The Ministry of Fear*, *This Gun for Hire*, *The Green Cockatoo/Four Dark Hours*).

Unlike the upper-class amateur detective of the British whodunit such as Sherlock Holmes, the hard-boiled detective in both British and American film noir is a working-class hero, a knight errant on a quest, and in the classical fiction of the 1920s through to the 1950s was invariably a man. Rather than assessing physical evidence, the detective spends most of his time conducting interviews (or fighting with enemies). Rather than solving crimes through logical deduction, he relies upon gut instinct. Also known as a private 'eye' or 'dick' the private detective offers a broad variety of services, including finding witnesses, missing persons, heirs or objects; investigating fraud; or conducting surveillance of cheating spouses. In reality, as David Wilt has observed, private detectives usually work for wealthy corporations, but the cinematic or televisual private eye is often employed by financially modest individuals (2003: 583). The private eye is an independent loner; tough, confident and self-contained, he is an intermediary between two worlds, the legal and the criminal, with skills and talents that enable him to operate in both. He is also a slob, a sexual loner and emotionally unattached; cynical and distrustful of women, he spends more time in his office than at home, because his work is his life.

The detective's quest usually centres on some kind of enigma, such as the search for a woman, whose identity or character usually proves to be unreliable (*Out of the Past*, *Laura*). In the course of this investigation, according to Martin Rubin, the detective faces three types of threats:

Fig. 6 'Can I trust her?': Philip Marlowe (Dick Powell) and Ann Grayle (Anne Shirley) in *Murder My Sweet*

physical, emotional and moral (1999: 194–6). Whereas the detective in the classic whodunit remains detached and cerebral, the private eye is always intimately (and physically) involved in the action. First, the detective is often suspected of murder by the police and is subject to their repeated interrogations, as well as to beatings from the criminals he meets along the way. These interrogations and beatings are so frequent as to be a leitmotif, underscoring noir's characteristic theme of male masochism. For example, in *Murder, My Sweet* Philip Marlowe (Dick Powell) is knocked unconscious three times, as well as drugged with a narcotic; as he ruefully remarks after another episode of unconsciousness, 'that old black pit opened up again, right on schedule'.

Second, the detective may become sexually involved with women, but these alliances are temporary, for he must always resist the lure of the femme fatale who would otherwise prove deadly. In fact, as Mary Ann Doane describes it, the femme fatale is someone who must be 'aggressively revealed, unmasked, discovered' in an act of masculine mastery (1991:

3). Oftentimes the detective is so obsessed with the femme fatale, that the crime story becomes secondary to her pursuit. In *Murder, My Sweet*, Marlowe ends up on two quests: first he is hired by ex-con Moose Malloy (Mike Mazurki) to find a woman named Velma Valento, and second he must figure out who killed another client of his named Marriott (Douglas Walton).

The plot revolves around an enigmatic femme fatale Mrs Helen Grayle (Clare Trevor) and the theft of her valuable jade necklace. Like many noirs, the femme fatale is juxtaposed with another 'good' woman, Ann Grayle (Anne Shirley), Helen Grayle's stepdaughter, but the moral distinction between the two is not always clear, and Marlowe regards both women with suspicion and cynicism. Unlike the hapless male protagonists of *Double Indemnity* or *The Postman Always Rings Twice*, the private detective ultimately resists the sexual lure of the femme fatale and survives. In *The Maltese Falcon*, Sam Spade (Humphrey Bogart) rejects femme fatale Brigid O'Shaughnessy (Mary Astor) and turns her in to the police, because she has murdered Miles Archer, and in Sam's mind, 'if a man's partner gets killed you're supposed to do something about it'. Rejecting her as much for the emotional power she has over him as for the crimes she has committed, Spade is typical of the noir detective who remains ultimately detached.

In addition to physical trials and sexual temptation, the detective must also face and resist moral temptation. In Chandler's words 'He is the hero, he is everything. He must be a complete man and a common man, and yet an unusual man. He must be … a man of honor, by instinct, by inevitability, without thought of it, and certainly without saying it' (1944: 54). In other words, the detective's personal character, rather than his achievements, is paramount. Although he may face sexual lures or monetary bribes he must reject them, as Marlowe does when Mrs Grayle tries to seduce him into killing her husband. Ultimately, the detective's quest is a journey which, by enduring physical punishment and sexual and moral temptation, enables him to better understand himself and his own values; as Marlowe wryly observes in *Murder, My Sweet*, 'I was hired as a bodyguard, but bungled the job. Now I'm investigating myself.'

The honorable Marlowe of the 1940s is in stark contrast to the 'bedroom detective' Mike Hammer (Ralph Meeker) in *Kiss Me Deadly* (1955), whose sociopathic character is an example of the increasingly bleak, paranoid and violent private eye of the late 1950s. In 1948, the Supreme Court decision in US v. Paramount ended Hollywood's monopoly over theatrical exhibition, and in the 1950s studios began to phase out the traditional double-bill in which low-budget film noirs were staples. As a new protagonist, the spy of Cold War thrillers began to replace the detective as hero, and the crime investigator would largely disappear for a decade, returning in the police film of the late 1960s.

The cinematic cop: from G Men to L.A. Confidential, 1935–2005

Police officers have been represented in cinema since its beginning, and on television since the late 1940s. Some of the earliest live television series were private eye shows like *Man Against Crime* (live 1949–52, recorded 1956) and *Martin Kane, Private Eye* (1949–54). In addition to the detached private eye, Nicole Rafter suggests that there have been two major cinematic stereotypes of law enforcement that have persisted in American cinema: the flatfoot Irish patrolman and the tough federal agent (2006: 112). The first type appeared in silent comedies like Buster Keaton's *Cops* (1922) and Mack Sennett's Keystone Cops series (1912–17), and later in television series like *The Blue Knight* (starring William Holden in 1973 and George Kennedy in 1975). The second type appeared in many Warner Bros. films of the 1930s such as *Let 'Em Have it* (1935), *Show Them No Mercy* (1935) and *You Can't Get Away With It* (1936). In *G Men* (1935), James Cagney is no longer the gangster he played in *The Public Enemy* but a poor young man raised by a mobster, who grows up to become a lawyer, and then a federal agent. After this, the federal agent largely disappears in cinema for over forty years, re-emerging as an FBI psychological profiler in serial killer films in the late 1980s and television shows in the 1990s and 2000s.

As a law enforcement official who restores order with a gun, the policeman and federal agent were closely related to the figure of the sheriff or Marshall in the western, which was one of the most popular genres in cinema and television in the 1950s. Martin Rubin suggests that in the 1970s the police film replaced the western as 'the most essential form of the American action film', with the plainclothes policeman replacing the gunslinger, the 44 Magnum the six-shooter, the car the horse, and the gritty modern city as the new Wild West frontier (1999: 140). This updating of the western's conventions are epitomised in a crossover police film, *Coogan's Bluff*, which was released in the same year as *Bullitt*, 1968. Clint Eastwood

plays Walt Coogan, an Arizona deputy sent to New York City to take possession of a prisoner who is being extradited to Arizona, but who escapes. A
'fish out of water' tale, Coogan is a lawman in Gotham City who uses his
western skills to recapture the escaped prisoner. The film's crossover elements are further reinforced by the casting of Eastwood, who first gained
fame as a star in the western television series *Rawhide* (1959–66), and who
went on to star in spaghetti westerns like *A Fistful of Dollars* (1964), and *The
Good, the Bad and the Ugly* (1966).

After the decline of film noir in the late 1950s, Hollywood returned to
the detective story in the late 1960s, with Paul Newman in *Harper* (1966)
and its sequel *The Drowning Pool* (1975), Frank Sinatra as *The Detective*
(1968), Richard Widmark as *Madigan* and Steve McQueen as *Bullitt*. Frank
Sinatra's *Tony Rome* (1967) was an insouciant, womanising detective
who had elements of Sinatra's 'rat pack' persona, and who would return
in *Lady in Cement* (1968). The Academy Award-winning *In the Heat of the
Night* (1967) was one of the first entries in the new police film of postclas-
sical Hollywood, in its story of a white racist Southern cop, Gillespie (Rod
Steiger), who finds common cause with Virgil Tibbs (Sidney Poitier), a black
Northern police officer who helps him solve a local homicide. Reflecting
the social upheavals of the US civil rights movement, the film was one of
the first to show a black police officer as hero, and to explicitly engage
with social issues like Southern racism. The roots of these films' protagonists were found in the tough-guy detectives of noir like Detective Wilson
(Robert Ryan) in *On Dangerous Ground* (1952) and Detective Sergeant Dave
Bannion (Glenn Ford) in *The Big Heat*. In fact, Foster Hirsch argues that the
police story of the late 1960s and early 1970s was an outgrowth of noir,
and that several crime films like *Odds Against Tomorrow* (1959), *Cape Fear*
(1962), *Experiment in Terror* (1962) and *The Manchurian Candidate* (1962)
are transitional noirs, in the fallow period between the end of classic noir
in the late 1950s and the beginning of neo-noir in the 1970s (1999: 145). He
suggests that the investigative formula of the detective film then expands
to include other character types, such as the criminal in *Point Blank* to a
surveillance expert (Gene Hackman) in *The Conversation* (1974), and a
journalist (Warren Beatty) in *The Parallax View* (1974), the latter two made
during the Watergate era. Another key investigator film of the early 1970s is
Serpico, which, atypically for the Watergate period, expresses optimism in
its real-life story of police officer Frank Serpico (Al Pacino) who, at the risk

of his own life, heroically exposed corruption in the NYPD. Meanwhile in the UK, *Sweeney!* (1976) and its sequel *Sweeney 2* (1978) featured maverick police officers Detective Inspector Jack Regan (John Thaw) and Detective Sergeant George Carter (Dennis Waterman). The *Sweeney* films were spin-offs of the eponymous television series (pilot 1974, series 1975–78), with their relentless characters partly influenced by the American rogue cop tradition, but, as Leon Hunt suggests, equally influenced by the seminal British revenge film *Get Carter*, in which a professional hitman (Michael Caine) is determined to avenge his brother's death (1999: 134).

A series of nostalgic American remakes and homages to the private eye of classic noir began in the 1970s with *Chandler* (1971) and *Farewell My Lovely* (1975), including Robert Altman's revisionist *The Long Goodbye* (1973), in which Detective Phillip Marlowe was reconceived as a shambling private investigator. Three key private investigator films of the 1970s, *Klute* (1971), *Chinatown* (1974) and *Night Moves* (1975), signalled the beginning of neo-noir. This time working in colour, neo-noir revised classic noir narratives by showing the detective or private investigator as unable to solve the crime, or avenge the victim. Thus, in *Chinatown*, although Jake Gittes (Jack Nicholson) solves the crime and identifies the villain as Noah Cross (John Huston) (who has committed incest with his own daughter, whom Cross kills), he gets away with his crimes, and Gittes is helpless to change anything. Similarly the conclusion of *Night Moves* shows the detective (Gene Hackman) helplessly wounded at the end. *Chinatown*, *Thunderbolt and Lightfoot* (1974) and *Dog Day Afternoon* (1975) were crime films that Todd Berliner calls 'genre benders', or 'films which exploit our habitual responses to generic conventions in order to set us up for their unconventional outcomes' (2001: 26). Unlike genre breakers like *The Long Goodbye*, which commented on the conventions of the detective story, these revisionist films were part of the New American Cinema of the 1970s, in which directors like Scorsese, Penn and Coppola reinvented classic genres like the police story and gangster film, but with a sharply more pessimistic tone.

By the 1980s, neo-noir emerged as the dominant form of the crime film with many remakes of classic noirs: *The Postman always Rings Twice* (1946, 1981) and *Kiss of Death* (1947, 1995); *Out of the Past* became *Against All Odds* (1984) and *The Big Clock* (1948) returned as *No Way Out* (1987); *Night and the City* (1950) was remade in 1992, *The Blue Gardenia* (1953) was remade as *The Morning After* (1986) and *A Kiss Before Dying* (1956) was remade in

1991. In the 1980s contemporary crime writers like Elmore Leonard became new sources for neo-noir with his *Rum Punch* adapted by Quentin Tarantino as *Jackie Brown* (1997), joining other Leonard adaptations by Steven Soderbergh (*Out of Sight*, 1998) and Barry Sonnenfeld (*Get Shorty*, 1995). Jim Thompson, whose story *The Getaway* was twice adapted to the screen (1972, 1994), was also the source for *The Killer Inside Me* (1976), *The Kill Off* (1989), *The Grifters* (1990) and *After Dark, My Sweet* (1990). Similarly, James Ellroy's novels were a popular source, from *Cop* (1988) to *L.A. Confidential* (1997) and *The Black Dahlia* (2006).

As part of the neo-noir cycle the private investigator or undercover police officer became more diverse with female and/or black detectives in *V.I. Warshawski* (1991), *Deep Cover* (1992) and *The Glass Shield* (1994). In *Devil in a Blue Dress* (1995), Ezekiel 'Easy' Rawlins (Denzel Washington) is both tough and sensitive, and unlike the classic noir private eye, strongly connected to domesticity and his local community. Neo-noir's deeply cynical or pessimistic portraits of the intractability of crime and corruption were evident in films like *Romeo is Bleeding*, *State of Grace* (1990) and *Bad Lieutenant* (1992), ultimately suggesting that there are no good cops. Similarly, Curtis Hanson's *L.A. Confidential* was an important neo-noir whose pessimistic story depicted widespread corruption and murderous deception in the police force. The rogue or corrupt cop developed during the 1960s, and later to largely replace the detective story, was a recurrent theme in neo-noir with *Ten to Midnight* (1983), *An Innocent Man* (aka *Hard Rain* (1989)), *Internal Affairs* (1989), *One Good Cop* (1991), *Unlawful Entry* (1992) and *Copland* (1997), and periodically counterpointed with the honest-cop film with *Witness* (1985) and *The Untouchables* (1987).

The end of the Production Code and the shift to the Ratings system for the first time enabled the extensive depiction of morally ambiguous police officers and graphically realistic violence. Like classic noir, the 1970s police film suggested an inextricable link between masculinity and competent law enforcement, suggesting that a good man always made a good police officer.

Typified by Clint Eastwood's Harry Callahan in *Dirty Harry* and Gene Hackman's Jimmy 'Popeye' Doyle in *The French Connection*, cops in this cycle were white, violent, rule-breaking, racist loose cannons, who used controversial methods to solve crime, and who were in constant conflict with their superiors and departments. These films suggested that the jus-

Fig. 7 The rise of the rogue cop in the 1970s: Clint Eastwood as Dirty Harry

tice system was deeply flawed, with criminals escaping justice through legal technicalities, and officers like Detective Leland (Frank Sinatra) in *The Detective* adopting violent strategies in response. In *Dirty Harry*, the eponymous Harry Callahan not only has garnered his nickname because he is racist, sexist and illegal in his policing tactics, but also because he gets 'every dirty job that comes along'. The film's story concerns Harry's illegal methods as he tries to hunt down a serial sniper named 'Scorpio' (Andy Robinson) who is killing people in San Francisco. Harry searches Scorpio's home without a warrant, and later tortures him and denies him access to a lawyer. When the district attorney (Josef Summer) berates Harry for his illegal actions, and refers to his violation of Escobedo v. Illinois (1964) and Miranda v. Arizona (1966), two recently-established precedents in constitutional law that allowed a defendant's right to full and free access to counsel, Harry retorts: 'Well I'm all broken up over that man's rights.' *Dirty Harry*, like the rogue cop cycle as a whole, appealed to an increasingly conservative American public who were anxious about high urban crime rates. Its trailer demonstrated the film's ambiguous marketing tactics, with a voice-over announcing, 'This is a movie about a couple of killers – Harry Callahan and a homicidal maniac. The one with the badge is Harry. You don't assign him to murder cases, you just turn him loose.' That Callahan is played by Eastwood, with his image as a loner fighting for justice, helps to reinforce him as an anit-hero, and strengthens the ways in which the film speaks to the audience's fears of rising crime and apparently soft sentencing, all deserving to be resolved by this renegade cop. Ultimately the film endorses Callahan's illegal methods in tracking down and killing Scorpio, with the enormous popularity of Dirty Harry's character spawning several sequels, including *Magnum Force* (1973), *The Enforcer* (1976) and *Sudden Impact* (1983).

The French Connection tells the true story of the biggest drug bust in New York City history when, in 1961, 112 pounds of pure heroin worth $32 million were seized by Detectives Eddie Egan and Sonny Grosso, fictionalised as 'Popeye' Doyle (Hackman) and 'Cloudy' Russo (Roy Scheider). Doyle's famous car chase (which, influenced by *Bullitt* (1968) and *The Getaway* (1972) went on to become an exciting new form of spectacle, and rapidly became a staple element in the police film) under the elevated subway line on Stillwell Avenue in Brooklyn shows his reckless disregard for the safety of pedestrians (a near miss with a woman with a pram), as does his indifference when he accidentally shoots a police agent Mulderig (Bill Hickman), and later deliberately shoots another man in the back. Other rogue cop films followed in the wake of *The French Connection* and *Dirty Harry*, including *Across 110th Street* (1972), *The Seven-ups* (1973), *The Laughing Policeman* (1973), *The Choirboys* (1977), *The Gauntlet* (1977), *The Black Marble* (1980) and *Cruising* (1980). This was also the era of Charles Bronson's *Death Wish*, which presented vigilantism sympathetically as a response to urban crime, and which also reflected the prominence of law and order issues in the 1968 and 1972 US presidential elections. The rogue cop films of this period could be seen as acting out a specific ideological message – a kind of wish fulfilment – in response to social fears of increased criminal disorder and failures of legal recourse.

In addition to the rogue cop film, a largely white-produced cycle of American action thrillers called 'blaxploitation' emerged in the 1970s, targeting African-American viewers as an underserved audience, and starring black heroes from Shaft (Richard Roundtree) to Coffy (Pam Grier). Whether as sexual superheroes ('Who's the black private dick that's a sex machine to all the chicks?') in Shaft, secret agents (*Cleopatra Jones* (1973), *Cleopatra Jones and the Casino of Gold* (1975)), female detectives (*Sheba Baby* (1975)), revenge films (*Foxy Brown* (1974)) and even cocaine-dealing anti-heroes (*Superfly*) (1972)), the American crime film was beginning to diversify and reflect the political and social changes of the Civil Rights and feminist movements. Outside the commercial world of blaxploitation, independent filmmakers like Ossie Davis with his adaptation of Chester Himes' *Cotton Comes to Harlem* (1970) and Melvin Van Peebles with *Sweet Sweetback's Baadasssss Song* (1971) show a further diversification of the crime film.

Linda Mizejewski's (2004) study of the female detective in fiction, film and television has shown us the pioneering role of the early TV series *Honey West* (1965–66), *Get Christie Love* (1974–75), *Police Woman* (1974–78) and *Charlie's Angels* (1976–81). Despite the sexism of these early shows (which emphasised the female detective's body as much as their work), these proto-feminist stories were an opportunity for television viewers to identify with and celebrate female crime fighters. By the 1990s, the female investigator was often found on British and American television and had become fully professionalised, with series like *Prime Suspect* (1991–93, 1995–96, 2003, 2006), and shows like *Under Suspicion* (1994–95), *The X-Files* (1993–2002) and *Profiler* (1996–2000) featuring female detectives or federal agents in lead roles, as well as important female supporting characters on ensemble shows like *Cold Case* (2003–present), and the *CSI* and *Law and Order* franchises. The female detective/police officer story had begun to appear more frequently in the cinema, too, from the 1980s, becoming a new variant of the cop film with *Fatal Beauty* (1987), *Black Widow* (1987), *Betrayed* (1988), *Impulse* (1990), *Blue Steel* (1990), *The Silence of the Lambs, Copycat, Fargo, Point of No Return*, aka *The Assassin*, 1993), *Out of Sight, Charlie's Angels* (2000) and its sequel *Charlie's Angels 2: Full Throttle* (2003), *Miss Congeniality* (2000), *Miss Congeniality 2: Armed and Fabulous* (2005) and *Hannibal* (2001). By the 1990s, the prominence of the female detective is epitomised in two Academy Award-winning performances: Jodie Foster as FBI agent Clarice Starling in *The*

Silence of the Lambs and Frances McDormand as Officer Marge Gunderson in *Fargo*.

The police film takes many generic forms in the 1980s, starting with the buddy cop comedy, which blended comedy with serious crime fighting in the humorous relationship of two partners, Eddie Murphy and Nick Nolte in *48 Hours* (1982) and *Another 48 Hours* (1990) and Mel Gibson and Danny Glover in the *Lethal Weapon* series (1987, 1989, 1992, 1998). Led by British Inspector Clouseau (Peter Sellers) and the influential *Pink Panther* series (various actors, 1963–2006), the comedy detective film was followed by American cop comedies like *Fuzz* (1972), *Flatfoot* (1973), *Fletch* (1985), *Raising Arizona* (1987) and *Ace Ventura: Pet Detective* (1994). The police comedy cycle particularly dominated the 1980s with *Police Academy* (1984, 1985, 1986, 1987, 1988, 1989, 1994), *Beverly Hills Cop* (1984) and its sequels (1987, 1994, 2009) and the *Naked Gun* spoof series (1988, 1991, 1994). These comedy cycles and spoofs foregrounded the hardened clichés of the police genre, and harkened back to the broad visual humour of Mack Sennett's Keystone Cops series of the teens and twenties, like *Bangville Police* (1913), by showing the police officer to be an incompetent buffoon. The buddy formula was also evident in serious crime dramas like *Colors* (1988), *The Rookie* (1990) and *Se7en*, and action thrillers like the *Die Hard* series (1988, 1990, 1995 and the next sequel due in 2007). Later variants on this formula paired a black male cop with a white female cop (*The Glass Shield*), *The Bone Collector* (1999)). In an Academy Award-winning performance as Alonzo Harris, Denzel Washington plays a corrupt undercover cop paired up with a rookie police officer (Ethan Hawke) in *Training Day* (2001), a film that blended the good cop/rogue cop and the buddy cop formula. Recalling classic noir films like *The Hitch-hiker*, ordinary situations like being at the office, on a bus, or at home become new narrative scenarios for crime stories of murder, robbery or kidnapping in contemporary crime thrillers like *Die Hard* and *Speed* (1994, sequel 1997).

An important new version of the crime film has emerged in the last decade, with comic book superheroes replacing crime fighting police officers and private eye films of the 1970s. The cycle has its roots in the movie serial of *The Batman* (1943) and *Batman and Robin* (1947) and also in the television series, *Batman* (1966–68), as well as in the ongoing theatrical releases of this superhero character (1989, 1992, 1995, 1997, 2005, 2008) as well as *Superman* (1978, 1980, 1983, 2006). The return of the comic book superhero was partly motivated by the increasing conglomeratisation of Hollywood that began in the 1970s and accelerated in the 1980s and 1990s. Turning to existing characters with built-in fan bases to guarantee audiences, media conglomerates created a cinematic cycle which includes *Judge Dredd* (1995), the *Blade* series (1998, 2002, 2004), *Inspector Gadget* (1999), *The Incredible Hulk* (filmed as *Hulk* in 2003, with the sequel in 2008), *Hellboy* (2004) and *The Fantastic Four* (2005, 2007). These films were hybrid genres, combining romance or comedy with the action film and a crime-fighting story. Related to this trend is the more recent turn to bestselling graphic novels as new sources for stories and presold characters, like Frank Miller's neo-noir American collection *Sin City* (1998) which became Robert Rodriguez's *Sin City* (2005, with two sequels in 2008), and John Wagner and Vince Locke's *A History of Violence*, which was adapted by David Cronenberg in 2005. Video games have continued to use crime as an organising narrative (particularly first-person shooter games like *Doom*), and a new trend is suggested in *The Godfather: The Game* (2006) in which players are invited to adopt characters from the classic 1972 film and navigate similar narrative scenarios to those found in the film and its sequels. Meanwhile, hybrids of the detective and science fiction genres, sometimes dubbed tech- or cyber noir, continued with *Blade Runner* (1982), *Dark City* and, more recently, the animated science fiction crime thrillers *A Scanner Darkly* (2006) and *Renaissance* (2006), which followed earlier classics like Jean-Luc Godard's *Alphaville* (1965). In Hollywood, thriller crime films like *Face/Off* (1997), *Minority Report* (2002) and *I Robot* (2004) blended science fiction with the action genre and crime story, and explored the relationship between technology, criminality and the body.

Another important cycle of crime films were independent documentaries, in which filmmakers like Errol Morris (*The Thin Blue Line* (1988)), Michael Moore (*Bowling for Columbine* (2002)), Nick Broomfield (*Aileen Wuornos: The Selling of a Serial Killer* (1992) and its sequel *Aileen: Life and Death of a Serial Killer* (2003)) become the crime investigators themselves, probing allegations of paedophilia in a family in *Capturing the Friedmans* (2003) and homophobic murder in *The Brandon Teena Story* (1997). In the 1970s, crime stories which focused on the victim had largely shifted from cinema into made-for-TV movies, and dramatised alcoholism, domestic abuse, eating disorders and other social issues raised by the feminist movement, although some cinematic examples of the victim film remained in *The*

Burning Bed (1984), *Dolores Claiborne* (1995), *The Accused* (1988) and *Boys Don't Cry* (1999). Following a cycle that included The Great Gambini (1937) and Miracles for Sale (1939), more recent films have also combined a narrative focus on the mysterious world of magicians with an element of crime, in *The Prestige* (2006) and *The Illusionist* (2006).

TV Cops 1950–2006

Since the 1950s the police story has been one of the most popular genres on television and has largely taken two forms: the ordinary bobby or patrolman on the beat, and the plainclothes detective. Starring Jack Webb as Joe Friday, the classic TV series *Dragnet* (1952–59, revived 1967–70) was a police procedural loosely based on the LAPD, or a story that emphasised the mundane drudgery of police work. Along with the western, the police story was one of the most popular genres on television with dozens of US series from *Highway Patrol* (1955–59), *Peter Gunn* (1958–61), *Naked City* (1958–63), *77 Sunset Strip* (1958–64), *The Detectives* (1959–62), *The Untouchables* (1959–63), *The F.B.I.* (1965–74) and *Adam-12* (1968–75). In Britain several long-running series about bobbies on the beat began with *Dixon of Dock Green* (1955–76) starring Jack Warner as George Dixon, in a role developed from the character he played in an earlier fiction film, the classic British crime drama *The Blue Lamp* (1949). Many British television series featured Scotland Yard detectives, such as *Fabian of the Yard* (1954–56) and the first British drama series shot on film, *No Hiding Place* (1959–67) and *Gideon's Way* (1964–66). Influenced by the American *Highway Patrol*, the BBC introduced the long running *Z Cars* (1962–78) which featured a faster narrative pace and increased social realism, with a documentary-like focus on modern policing methods, and a shift away from the individual bobby on the beat to the mobile police team. Set in the fictional Newtown, the producers stated that one of the series' objectives was to explore ordinary people's lives in Northwest England and its popularity led to a spin-off, *Softly, Softly* (1966–69, then retitled *Softly, Softly: Task Force*, 1969–76) (see Cooke 2001).

Led by the James Bond films starring Sean Connery, the spy genre dominated the 1960s, and television soon followed with shows like *The Man From U.N.C.L.E.* (1964–68). Offering a new variant on the detective formula by injecting class and wealth, the American *Burke's Law* (1963–66, revived

1994), like *Batman*, starred a crime-fighting millionaire, here named Amos Burke (Gene Barry). Responding to the social turmoil of the 1960s, *The Mod Squad* (1968–73) was a new kind of police series about three former juvenile delinquents who were recruited by the police department to become under-cover cops. *The Streets of San Francisco* (1972–77) paired a wise older cop (veteran actor Karl Malden) with a youthful Michael Douglas. Meanwhile, the tradition of the classic whodunit detective continued in *Columbo* with the eponymous detective in a rumpled raincoat, carefully masking his sharp deductive skills with a subterfuge of ticks, twitches and tangents. Other variants on the detective story included Raymond Burr as, respectively, a defence attorney in the long-running series *Perry Mason* (1957–66) and the disabled Chief of Detectives in *Ironside* (1967–75); Dennis Weaver as the western lawman in *McCloud* (1970–77); and James Franciscus as an insur-ance investigator in *Longstreet* (1971–72).

In the 1970s the British television police series shifted back to a focus on individual police officers and detective inspectors with *The Sweeney* and continued in the next three decades with *Inspector Morse* (1987–93; specials 1995–2000), *The Inspector Alleyn Mysteries* (1990–94), *A Touch of Frost* (1992–present), *Cracker* (UK 1993–96, US 1997–98), *The Inspector Lynley Mysteries* (2001–present) and *Touching Evil* (UK 1997–99, US 2004). Other British detective shows included *The Chinese Detective* (1981–82), *Bergerac* (1981–91) and a Scottish detective, *Taggart* (1983–present). Some of these shows demonstrated a move away from the obvious set-tings of the Southern metropolis: *Bergerac* was set on the island of Jersey and *Taggart* in Glasgow. There was also a mix of classes, more typical of the British police show, with Detective Inspector Lynley belonging to the upper classes, assisted by the working class Detective Sergeant Havers, and Inspector Morse's pretensions to the middle classes evidenced by his love of classical music, gently ridiculed by his more working-class partner, DS Lewis. The central characters of *Cracker* and *Touching Evil* demonstrated educated awareness in the face of police distrust of what was perceived as intellectualism over experience.

Both American and British television police dramas were of two basic types. The first type featured eccentric, rebellious outsiders (*Mod Squad*, *Mannix* (1967–75), *Hawaii-Five-O* (1968–80), *Cannon* (1971–76), *McMillan and Wife* (1971–76), *Columbo*, *Kojak* (1973–78), *Baretta* (1975–1978), *Starsky and Hutch* (1975–79), *Jigsaw John* (1976)), and were influenced by the Hollywood police procedural. The second type were realistic dramas about police work: in the US (*Police Story* (1973–77), *The Blue Knight* (1975–76), *Hill Street Blues* (1981–87)), and in the UK *The Bill* (1984–present), its spin-off *M.I.T.: Murder Investigation Team* (2003–present), *Between the Lines* (1992–94), *The Cops* (1998–2001) and *City Central* (1998–2000). In addition there were hybrid shows, from police comedies (*Barney Miller* (1975–82), *The Misadventures of Sheriff Lobo*, later renamed *Lobo* (1979–81), *Police Squad* (1982, later leading to the *Naked Gun* films), to fantasy shows (*Knightrider* (1982–86) and *Automan* (1983–84)) (see Inciardi & Dee 1987: 95–6). More recently, following the success of *The Silence of the Lambs* and the *CSI* franchise, other shows featuring psychological profilers, psychics and other investigative characters have appeared (*Profiler* (1996–2000), *Cold Case*, *Medium* (2005–present) and *Criminal Minds* (2005–present)).

The premiere of *Hill Street Blues* in 1981 was a seminal moment in American police drama, as it initiated an influential formula that has been widely copied in series like *Homicide: Life on the Street* (1993–99, TV movie 2000), *NY Undercover* (1994–98), *Third Watch* (1999–2005), *The Shield* (2002–present) and *The Wire* (2002–present). *Hill Street Blues* was an ensemble show that balanced stories of police officers' personal and professional lives. Its large multiethnic cast pioneered other innovations including overlapping dialogue, a complex narrative structure with multi-week narrative arcs and documentary-style camerawork. Following this, *NYPD Blue* (1993–2005) also injected new standards of realism through changes in language and nudity practices in order to compete with new cable channels like HBO and F/X. Following the social changes of the feminist movement of the 1970s more female police officers or detectives became part of precinct shows like *Hill Street Blues*, *CSI*, *NYPD Blue* and *Third Watch*. Starring Angie Dickinson as Sergeant Suzanne 'Pepper' Anderson, *Police Woman* (1974–78) was one of the first American shows to feature a female character in the lead investigative role, and was followed by *Cagney and Lacey* (1982–88) in the US, while the first British show to feature a female police inspector, *The Gentle Touch* (1980–84), was followed four months later by another with *Juliet Bravo* (1980–85). These pioneering shows influenced subsequent programmes like *Wolcott*, the first show to feature a black female detective (1981), *Prime Suspect* and *Rosemary and Thyme* (2003–present).

Three major developments in the crime genre occurred in America in the early 1990s: the emergence of the first 24-hour cable television channel solely devoted to crime; the emergence of tabloid television programming and reality shows, and the proliferation of top-rated fictional nighttime crime series devoted to social issues around crime and punishment. Court TV, the new 24-hour network started by Steven Brill, began operation in 1991, but it was not until the sensational trial of brothers Lyle and Erik Menendez (who were accused of murdering their parents with a shotgun on 20 August 1989), that Court TV's ratings took off, as the trial ran from July 1993 to January 1994. Together with the O. J. Simpson trial in 1995, live courtroom coverage became a national obsession. Enabled by a Supreme Court decision in 1981 which permitted cameras in the courtroom for the first time, televised trials, like fictional television series, offered the suspense of the jury's verdict, the drama of the adversarial system, in which prosecutors and defence attorneys offered competing narratives of the crime, the graphic sensationalism and gory details of violence, and a melodramatic cast of characters from defendants to lawyers, judges, juries, witnesses and forensic psychiatrists.

In 1988 with the cooperation of the FBI, two influential new crime shows debuted. *Unsolved Mysteries* (1987–2002) and *America's Most Wanted* (1988–present) featured re-enactments of unsolved crimes, and solicited the public's help with cases and fugitive criminals. They were rapidly followed by *Cops* (1989–present), *LAPD: Life on the Beat* (1995) and *American Bounty Hunter* (1996) (the latter formula was also examined in Tony Scott's film *Domino* (2005)). Rather than following the crime drama's traditional narrative arc of crime, investigation and punishment, *Cops* followed a serial rather than series format, presenting six or seven cases in a 22-minute show, often involving drunkenness, domestic abuse and minor altercations, and set in a metaphoric borderland of trailer parks and working-class and immigrant communities in smalltown America. As television critic Elayne Rapping has observed, the framing, vérité use of police tapes or documentary interviews and editing techniques of shows like *Cops* decontextualise the actions of the petty 'criminals' suggesting a conservative portrait in which the police are a heroic blue line between the social chaos of criminality and the public (2003: 55–60).

The franchises of *Law and Order* (1990–present) with three spin-offs, *Law and Order: Special Victims Unit* (1999–present), *Law and Order:*

Criminal Intent (2001–present) and *Law and Order: Trial by Jury* (2005–06), and *CSI* (with two spin-offs) were matched by new cable shows that adopted gritty stories about urban crime (*Homicide: Life on the Street*, *The Wire*), corrupt cops (*The Shield*), prisons (*Oz*) or skilful genre hybrids such as the enormously popular *The Sopranos* (1999–2007) which blended the traditional gangster story with pop psychology and therapeutic discourse.

Many of these shows demonstrate a complex response to crime and the criminal: they are often morally ambiguous with no clear demarcation between police officer and criminal. Similar to the rogue cop films of the 1960s and 1970s, they show that the justice system is fighting corruption and economic problems and that traditional methods of law enforcement are not working. Plots, narrative structures and visual style are often cinematic and more experimental than television usually allows for. Plots can develop over whole series, and as an audience we are placed in positions where we can question our own morality and expectations of law enforcement. We can see that prison, as in *Oz*, dehumanises the inmates and exacerbates already critical situations. In many ways these groundbreaking shows are a creative and artistic response to increasingly conservative developments in American law and order.

Beginning under the Reagan Presidency, and intensifying under Bill Clinton and George W. Bush, the United States became increasingly conservative about matters of law and order (although public perceptions about escalating crime rates did not reflect reality, as crime had been steadily declining since the 1980s). Together with a new victims' rights movement, the reinstitution of the death penalty in many states and a rise in incarceration rates and prison construction which have led to the largest prison population in the world, Americans supported ever more punitive legislative approaches to crime, including Clinton's 'three strikes and you're out' sentencing policy. As Rapping observes, this trend is paralleled by the shift from the early liberalism of *Law and Order*'s first few seasons in the 1990s with Ben Stone (Michael Moriarty) as the Assistant DA, to the more conservative Jack McCoy (Sam Waterston) of recent years. Reality television, 24-hour cable and night time crime dramas exemplified what Rapping describes as a 'widespread national tendency to define and approach all social issues and problems within the narrow terrain of criminal law' (2003: 17). That is, the most commercially popular legal shows in the US in the 1990s like *The*

Practice (1997–2004) and *Law and Order* became a social forum in which to stage debates over controversial social issues like juvenile crime, the death penalty, mental illness, and so on, but which always framed these issues in moral rather than legal terms.

The moral didacticism of the American television crime drama echoes earlier moral melodramas in the crime tradition dating back to Griffith's *Musketeers of Pig Alley*. *Law and Order* in particular emphasises the institution of criminal justice and over the course of the last 17 years has featured dozens of actors in interchangeable roles as police officers, district attorneys or judges who enforce the law. Unlike in the police shows *NYPD Blue* or *The Shield*, personal lives remain off-screen, and each character's institutional role is emphasised over their private lives (Rapping 2003: 46). *Law and Order* follows an invariable formula, with the first half-hour of the show dedicated to the police investigation which begins with the discovery of the body, and the second half-hour with the trial and jury verdict. At the end of each show, suspense is created through the musical score which features an anticipatory string motif and drum beats, usually combined with zoom-ins to the faces of the defendants, lawyers and jurors as the verdict is announced. Unlike the private eye of film noir, police officers like Lenny Briscoe (Jerry Orbach) are part of the system, and not intermediaries between law and crime. However, like the hard-boiled private eye, protagonists like DA Jack McCoy and Officer Briscoe are loners and drinkers; dysfunctional men with little life outside their jobs.

As Susanna Lee suggests, *Law and Order* represents a fantasy response to violence: its focus is on how humans respond to crime as much as with the crime itself, combining the representation of violence with the assurance that someone (the social justice system) is always watching and shaping it into narrative form. Like the classic amateur detective film, the TV crime show has, according to Lee, 'always represented both the desire for reassurance and the simultaneous sense of the impossibility of that reassurance' (2003: 81). Unlike the earlier gangster films of the 1930s, in which good triumphed over evil, and the criminal ended up imprisoned or dead, on television we frequently see shows which lack closure just like real life: cases remain unsolved, murderers go free and innocent people are imprisoned. Instead, the crime show provides a resolution that is psychic rather than social (Rapping 2003: 89). Unlike the defence attorneys on *The Practice*, who are progressively undone by their ethical ambivalence about their jobs, the cops and attorneys in *Law and Order* remain cynical yet detached, and impervious yet determined.

Unlike *Cops*, but like many classic films noir, *Law and Order* and several other contemporary crime dramas depict criminals as morally closer to the viewing audience, divided only by the actions of a moment of passion. Unlike earlier television crime dramas of the 1950s, the dividing line between good and bad is no longer so clearly drawn. In the next chapter, we shall see that this moral ambiguity is a recurrent theme in the erotic thriller, courtroom drama and neo-noir of recent contemporary film.

3   THE CRIMINAL I: EROTIC THRILLERS, NEO-NOIR
     AND TRIAL FILMS

The erotic thriller and neo-noir

Beginning in the 1970s, and accelerating in the 1980s and 1990s, Hollywood made a series of thrillers whose themes and visual style echoed the classic era of film noir. Known as 'neo-noir', this crime cycle included stories about heists, outlaw lovers, innocent bystanders, private eyes, femmes fatales and relatively new character types, the hit man and serial killer. Unlike classic noir, films like *Red Rock West* (1992), *Fargo* and *U Turn* (1997) were set in small towns, rural communities and Southwestern landscapes, rather than cities. Although these films emulated the chiaroscuro lighting and stylised *mise-en-scène* of classic noir, they were photographed in colour rather than black and white (one important exception was Joel and Ethan Coen's *The Man Who Wasn't There* (2001). Like classic noir, neo-noir included many erotic thrillers in which the central protagonist becomes sexually ensnared by a charismatic criminal, and led into a suspenseful and mortally dangerous situation, but sometimes the charismatic criminals were *hommes fatals*, in *Betrayed, Jagged Edge* (1985) and *Masquerade* (1988).

Three key films marked the emergence of the neo-noir erotic thriller: *Body Heat, Fatal Attraction* and *Basic Instinct*, which will be looked at in more detail in this chapter. These seminal films were enormously influential, spurring the production of *Final Analysis* (1992), *Sliver* (1993) and *The Last Seduction* (1994), amongst others. In particular, Julianne Pidduck has suggested that *Fatal Attraction* produced a separate but related group of films that she calls the *fatal femme* cycle, including *The Hand that Rocks* the Cradle (1992) and The Temp (1993), in which psychotic, destructive female antagonists are violently eliminated by the end of the film (Pidduck 1995: 64–72). Also overlapping with what Barry Keith Grant has called the 'yuppie horror movie', or thrillers like Pacific Heights (1990) and Bad Influence (1990) which specifically addressed the 'anxieties of an affluent culture in an era of prolonged recession', the erotic thriller shares with the horror film the central narrative element of violence, and by anticipating yet deferring this violence, creates suspense (1998: 280). Consequently, like the cop film, suspense rather than mystery is a key element of the erotic thriller. Like pornography, the erotic thriller also entices the specta- tor with a marketing 'come-on', appealing to the viewer's voyeurism with sexual scenes (Williams 1993). Like the horror film, the erotic thriller trades on our ambivalent desire and dread of violence. The storylines of many erotic thrillers use controversial subjects like bisexuality (Basic Instinct), sexual harassment (Disclosure (1994)) and the sex industry (Striptease (1996)) as marketing devices to pique viewer interest (Feasey 2003: 167), although the subjects of some of these films can also be considered as a response to the fear of stong, sexually-confident women and the apparent 'demotion' of masculine power. The erotic thriller emphasises the person- ality and motivation of the criminal, who usually manipulates through their personal and/or sexual charisma, and who threatens a nuclear family. Unlike the horror film, this threat to the family is initially veiled, but in the narrative's suspenseful climax, the homme fatal or femme fatale are finally killed. According to Andrew McKenna, another defining character- istic of the erotic thriller is that the viewer's identification is 'strategically confused between pursuer and pursued'; that is, we identify visually and narratively with both victim and stalker, and this 'oscillation is the essence of suspense' (1996: 227, 230).

Sabrina Barton has identified a sub-genre of the erotic thriller which she calls the female psychothriller, in which women are terrorised or attacked by a male criminal, in Positive ID (1987), Deceived (1991), Shattered (1991), Consenting Adults (1992), Copycat, Eye for an Eye (1996), Double Jeopardy (1999) and What Lies Beneath (2000). However, unlike most erotic thrill- ers, the female psychothriller has a female protagonist who controls the narrative and camera's point of view. In films like The Stepfather (1987), The Silence of the Lambs and Sleeping with the Enemy (1991), she inves- tigates a male character who is duplicitous (often with a false identity), and in the process reinforces her own sense of self (2002: 189–90). Unlike Gothic women's pictures like *Rebecca* and *Suspicion*, in which the female protagonist's suspicions about her husband were revealed to be errone-ous or pathological, the psychothriller of the 1980s and 1990s ultimately endorses the female protagonist's misgivings, showing that she must shoot her violent husband or boyfriend as an act of self-defence in *Lipstick* (1976), *Sleeping With the Enemy* and *Enough* (2002).

Sex

The explicit sex scenes and partial nudity of *Body Heat* epitomised the erotic thriller's focus on 'the enticements and perils of lust' (Hirsch 1999: 179). Enabled by the end of the Production Code and the shift to the ratings system in 1968, sex and nudity could now be shown on American screens. Moreover the invention of video recording technology in the 1970s changed social viewing practices, and as Linda Ruth Williams' recent study of the erotic thriller and pornography shows, led to an economic explosion in the production of films which featured sexual context, or in the case of the erotic thriller, fused both sex and violence (2005: 3). In the 1970s second-wave feminism had also transformed gender roles, and the widespread availability and legality of contraception and abortion also enabled sexual freedoms, such that the erotic thriller now featured female characters who were both career professionals and active and desiring sexual agents. Yet the politics of these crime films often revealed deep male anxieties about female sexual empowerment and agency, reflecting the increasingly con-servative social turn and backlash against feminism in the United States that began under Reagan in the 1980s. Many critics have pointed out that this sexual conservatism is connected to a longstanding sexual Puritanism in American culture, which accelerated in the 1980s in the wake of the AIDS epidemic, and as *Fatal Attraction*'s title implies, suggested that a woman's sexual desire was murderous, and the consequences of extra-marital sex, fatal. These conservative sexual politics echo those of the influential early erotic thriller *Dressed to Kill* (1980) which suggested that sexual promiscu-ity (especially for women) must be punished. Yet unlike the traditional pun-ishment meted out to classic noir's femme fatale, who usually died along with her male victim in films like *Out of the Past*, the erotic thriller often showed the femme fatale getting away with her crimes, as in *Final Analysis*

(1992), while her male victim ended up in jail or dead, as in *Body Heat*. So powerful were the femmes fatales of the neo-noir/erotic thriller, with vampiric monsters like Mona Demarkov (Lena Olin) in *Romeo is Bleeding*, and Bridget Gregory (Linda Fiorentino) in *The Last Seduction*, that the female criminal bordered on the supernatural. The neo-noir cycle also equated homosexuality with criminal psychopathology (*Basic Instinct, Single White Female*) or made lesbianism into the new narrative frisson, either implicitly, in the homoerotic bond between investigator (Debra Winger) and killer (Theresa Russell) in *Black Widow* (1987), or explicitly, in the heroic duo who become lovers in *Bound* (1996). Variations on the erotic thrillers like *Still of the Night* (1982) and *China Moon* (1994) also played with classic noir archetypes of the criminal femme fatale by creating characters that ultimately turn out to be innocent, like Helen Cruger (Ellen Barkin) in *Sea of Love* (1989).

One star who frequently played the protagonist victim of the neo-noir erotic thriller is Michael Douglas, who is sexually harassed by a woman in *Disclosure*; stalked by a woman unsatisfied that their sexual encounter is limited to a one night stand in *Fatal Attraction;* and seduced and manipulated by a bisexual who may be a killer in *Basic Instinct*. The erotic thriller's combination of sex and violence has also continued to be an important staple driving the careers of actresses like Sharon Stone (*Basic Instinct, Sliver, Diabolique* (1996), *Basic Instinct 2* (2006)), Demi Moore (*Mortal Thoughts* (1991), *Indecent Proposal* (1993) and *Disclosure)* and Ashley Judd (*Double Jeopardy, Kiss the Girls* (1997), *Eye of the Beholder* (1999), *Along Came a Spider* (2001), *High Crimes* (2002)), as well as Jennifer Lopez (*U Turn, The Cell* (2000), *Angel Eyes* (2001), *Bordertown* (2007)), Theresa Russell (*Black Widow, Physical Evidence* (1989)), Lena Olin (*Romeo is Bleeding*), Linda Fiorentino (*The Last Seduction, Jade* (1995)), Lara Flynn Boyle (*Eye of the Storm* (1991), *Red Rock West, The Temp* (1993)), Joanne Whalley-Kilmer (*Kill Me Again*, (1989), Kim Basinger (*The Getaway, L. A. Confidential, Final Analysis, Cellular* (2004), *While She Was Out* (2008)) and Annette Bening (*The Grifters*). Another key creative figure associated with this crime cycle is screenwriter Joe Eszterhas, author of *Basic Instinct* and *Basic Instinct 2*, as well as *Jagged Edge, Betrayed, Sliver, Jade* and *Showgirls* (1995). In most of his films, criminals are female, and protagonists are male victims. Let us now take a closer look at the erotic thriller that initiated this formula.

Body Heat

'She'll fuck me to death', says Ned Racine (William Hurt) of Matty Walker (Kathleen Turner), the married woman with whom he is sexually obsessed. Although this does not quite come true, Ned's lust for Matty does lead to sexual entrapment, murder and his lifetime imprisonment for her crimes. Following the classic noir formula of *Double Indemnity*, *Body Heat* is a story in which a femme fatale seduces a man into killing her husband. As a reworking of a classic noir tale, it also links sex with crime and death. In response to Matty's voracious sexual appetite, her husband's joking question 'are you trying to kill me?' foreshadows his subsequent murder by Ned. Unlike classic noir, however, Matty lives to enjoy the fruits of her crimes. Repeatedly warned that 'you're no genius' by his friends, Ned is so besotted with Matty that he kills her husband only to discover he has been double-crossed through a fake will she has written. Matty inherits all her husband's money, and Ned goes to jail for Walker's murder. Deception, manipulation and false identities are leitmotifs in the erotic thriller. As Ned sits in jail in the film's closing shots, he opens Matty's high school year book to discover that her real name was Mary Ann Simpson, and that she had killed the original Matty Walker (née Tyler) and taken over

Fig. 8 She'll fuck me to death': Matty Walker (Kathleen Turner) and Ned Racine (William Hurt) in *Body Heat*

her identity as part of her high school ambition 'to be rich on an exotic island'. Not unlike the homme fatal Jack Forrester (Jeff Bridges) in *Jagged Edge*, Matty is a sociopath of uncommon cunning, who has systematically planned her crimes over many years; yet because *Body Heat* frames its story through the eyes of Ned Racine, she remains enigmatic and ambiguous, an essentially unknowable yet devious criminal. *Body Heat* was influential in several ways. The steamy sex is not only explicitly depicted but metaphorically suggested in the story's title and setting, for the absence of air-conditioning and the ubiquitous humidity (humorously parodied in Carl Reiner's *Fatal Instinct* (1993)) leads the characters to sweat profusely, and also suggests the physicality of sexual desire and its languid aftermath. The recklessness that sexual desire prompts is suggested in a scene in which Ned breaks a glass window in order to get into Matty's home, whereupon they promptly have sex on the floor. Like many later erotic thrillers, the film suggests that sexual desire is irresistibly compulsive and implicitly leads to moral recklessness and criminal behaviour. *Body Heat*'s explicit sex scenes updated classic noir for the 1980s, reflecting both the greater sexual freedoms of the contemporary age, but also profound social ambivalence over sex catalysed by the AIDS era (Leitch 2002: 152). Much of this social ambivalence becomes projected onto the femme fatale. As the castrating woman she becomes the object of blame, and as we see with our next erotic thriller, she becomes such a threat to the family that she must be annihilated.

Fatal Attraction

The story of married couple Dan (Michael Douglas) and Beth Gallagher (Anne Archer), and Alex Forrest (Glenn Close), *Fatal Attraction* is a classic triangle story. Like many erotic thrillers, this film sets up an opposition between the safe yet boring domestic world of the family and the exciting yet dangerous realm of the sexual. Dan Gallagher meets Alex at a work party, is attracted to her and has (what he assumes will be) a one night stand. As is typical of the female characters in the erotic thriller, Alex is sexually assertive. She openly returns Dan's gaze of sexual interest, prompting his friends to say 'if looks could kill…', foreshadowing just how dangerous she will become. An unmarried, childless professional, Alex is coded as outside the domestic sphere, and from her androgynous name to her home in New York City's meat market district, Alex typifies the femme fatale's profound symbolic threat to the nuclear family and marriage. When Alex becomes upset about Dan's brush-off after their sexual encounter, he says to her, 'You knew the rules.' Not accepting these rules, Alex discovers she is pregnant, and refuses to have an abortion. Ultimately Alex wishes to replace Dan's wife, and as she points out to him, his infidelity already suggests dissatisfaction in his marriage.

When Alex and Dan initially have passionate, rough sex, they knock over furniture and end up at the kitchen sink. Their aggressive lovemaking foreshadows the violence that will later erupt between them, and also underscores the close relationship between sex and violence in the erotic thriller. This scene is recalled later when Dan is outraged by Alex's threats to his family and nearly strangles her at that same sink. Increasingly Alex intrudes on Dan's space, first calling him at his office, and then at home, and finally makes a surprise visit to his house. Similarly, her actions become progressively more threatening (she throws acid on his car, kidnaps his daughter, Ellen (Ellen Hamilton Latzen), and takes her to an amusement park, and, in a notorious scene, kills and cooks Ellen's pet rabbit). Crosscutting in two key scenes increases narrative tension. The first is when Beth Gallagher comes home to discover that her daughter's rabbit is cooking on the stove. Beth's puzzled approach to the cooking pot is crosscut with a low-angle steadicam shot which tracks her daughter Ellen as she runs outside to see her rabbit in its cage. The two characters are linked by screams as Beth realises what is in the pot, and Ellen screams that her rabbit is missing. Similarly, in a second scene, as Beth frantically searches for her daughter at school, we crosscut to an amusement park where we see that Alex has taken Ellen on a rather scary rollercoaster ride.

Director Adrian Lyne plays with conventions of costume, as Alex shifts from wearing black clothing (when she is Dan's object of desire) to white clothing (when she becomes violent to herself, and to Dan), and increasingly becomes more dishevelled, with her make-up running and her hair askew. Although Dan tries to kill Alex twice, it is Beth who finally shoots her in the film's climax, as Alex rises out of the bath (in which she had apparently drowned) like a character in a horror film. This scene reveals the close relationship between the erotic thriller and the horror genre, in which Beth fulfills the traditional role of what Carol Clover calls the 'final girl', or the surviving female character in the slasher horror film who will ultimately dispatch the monster (1992: 35). More horror film than neo-noir, with a mentally disturbed stalker as its villain, *Fatal Attraction* pathologises the independent, sexual woman, constructing her as a psychotically violent monster who must be killed to protect the sanctity of the Gallaghers' marriage. Like *Body Heat*, it tells its story from the perspective of a male protagonist, inviting the viewer to empathise with Dan's plight. Whereas *Fatal Attraction* presents Alex Forrest's criminality as rooted in personal psychopathology, our third case study presents a more complex and ambiguous relationship between criminal and protagonist, suggesting that there is less distance between the two than we might think.

Basic Instinct

After a decade of small parts in TV and films, Sharon Stone got her first big break as an assassin in *Total Recall* (1990) but her breakthrough role to stardom was as *Basic Instinct*'s Catherine Tramell, a wealthy bisexual writer who may kill her male lovers as she has sex with them. Nick 'Shooter' Curran (Michael Douglas) is a detective investigating the murder of a rock star, Johnny Boz (Bill Cable), who comes to both sleep with and suspect Catherine as the killer. A former alcoholic and cocaine addict, Curran has accidentally killed four civilians in five years, and like 'Dirty' Harry, he is in trouble with Internal Affairs, which views him as 'out of control'. His partner Gus Moran (George Dzundza) scolds Nick, and suggests that 'you [are] still feeling so bad about [killing the civilians] you're wiggling your way into an ice pick'. Catherine manipulates Nick throughout. When he tries to follow her in his car, their chase through the hills outside of San Francisco is a metaphor for their sexual chase. He asks Tramell what book she is currently working on and she tells him it is about a detective – 'He falls for the wrong woman.' When Nick asks her 'what happens' she replies 'she kills him'. Even more so than the passive and masochistic male characters that become ensnared in the sexual coils of the femme fatale in classic noir films like *The Killers*, *Basic Instinct* intensifies the gender role-reversal of the male and female characters in the erotic thriller. Referring to Tramell Gus tells Nick that that 'magna cum laude pussy done fried your brain', and that Nick's belief that Catherine is innocent is 'your pussy talking', thereby suggesting that being sexually obsessed with the femme fatale is an act of male masochism which ultimately feminises men. As Steven Cohan says of

Catherine Tramell, 'she, not the male, is active, empowered to take charge of the narrative because of her intelligence, whereas he, not the female, is passive, victimised by her in the narrative because of his passion' (1998: 273). Indeed, later we see Nick submit as Catherine ties him up in a similar way to Johnny Boz, as they have sex. Completely helpless and at her mercy, Nick is aroused by their ambiguous role-playing, calling Catherine 'the fuck of the century'.

When Nick goes to Tramell's house to question her, he first sees a beautiful young blonde descend the staircase, in a scene that alludes to the first appearance of Phyllis Dietrichson (Barbara Stanwyck) in one of the classic noir period's most famous erotic triangle/crime stories, *Double Indemnity*. However, the beautiful blonde turns out to be Roxy (Leilani Sarelle), Catherine's lesbian lover. Like many neo-noirs, *Basic Instinct* adopts the stylised cinematography of classic noir, with prominent shadows cast by Venetian blinds notable in two key scenes; the first is in Beth Garner's (Jeanne Tripplehorn) office, and the second, in the film's infamous interrogation scene of Catherine Tramell. In the latter, low camera angles and swish pans complement an editing sequence in which the camera cuts back and forth between Catherine and the police interrogator's respective points of view. At first this scene seems to suggest classic Hollywood editing practices which align narrative and visual points of view, in which the male protagonist looks with the camera, and the female character is, in Laura Mulvey's words 'to be looked at' (1999: 487). However, Tramell defiantly invites the male gaze by opening her legs in *Basic Instinct*'s notorious crotch shot. By self-reflexively offering herself up as enigmatic spectacle, she underlines her agency and challenges Nick and the other officers to acknowledge their own desires. The editing and camera movement of this scene are later echoed when Nick is interrogated about the mysterious murder of another detective, whom he had threatened earlier. Like Tramell, Nick lights a cigarette, and when told that smoking is not allowed echoes Catherine's defiant words, 'What are you going to do? Arrest me for smoking?' This formal parallelism suggests that Nick has crossed over into Catherine's world, and shortly thereafter, they sleep together. Typical of many neo-noirs, *Basic Instinct* makes a series of self-reflexive thematic and visual allusions to earlier erotic thrillers, and especially to Alfred Hitchcock's *Vertigo*. Like *Basic Instinct*, *Vertigo* is a story about a detective obsessed with a woman whose identity is ambiguous, and Verhoeven underscores the connection between the films by having Catherine Tramell wear dresses which are exact replicas of those worn by Madeleine in Hitchcock's film.

Tramell repeatedly challenges Nick about his drinking and cocaine habits, and also comments sarcastically on the frequency of his accidental shooting deaths, sardonically using his nickname ('but you know all about homicidal impulse, don't you Shooter?'). As Nick questions Tramell about her friendship with murderer Hazel Dobkins (Dorothy Malone), and the suspicious death of her psychology professor Noah Goldstein at Berkeley, she throws back each question with another, suggesting that he is morally compromised, and that he disavows his own desires (to drink, to kill), and that he actually 'liked it'. Tramell invites Curran's sexual interest, but as it later turns out, her seduction of Nick was merely a performance for her lover Roxy, who watched their lovemaking through a two-way mirror. Referring to the fact that they each have passed polygraph tests, Catherine sarcastically observes, 'You see, we're both innocent Nick.'

Not only is Nick ethically compromised, the film suggests that his association with Tramell's 'deviant sexuality' only further corrupts him. At the time of its release *Basic Instinct* was boycotted by various gay rights organisations for its equation of homosexuality and criminal pathology, but other critics argued that Verhoeven's thematic concerns with sex and death were longstanding dimensions of his work, going back to his film *The Fourth Man* (1983). *Basic Instinct*'s narrative emphasis on Tramell's bisexuality, and on explicit and graphic scenes of raw sexuality, is another way in which it marketed itself as an erotic and controversial thriller. In order to avoid the NC-17 rating and retain the more marketable rating of R, cuts were made which disguised the explictness of two sex scenes (when Nick has oral sex with Tramell and anal sex with ex-girlfriend Beth Garner).

Beth turns out to have her own longstanding fixation with Catherine Tramell, which dates back to their years together at university. Wearing a blonde wig, her murder of Nick's partner Gus in the elevator is an allusion to Brian De Palma's *Dressed to Kill*, which famously featured the murder of Angie Dickinson in an elevator by a transsexual in a blonde wig (Michael Caine), and as with the film's allusions to Hitchcock are another way in which its generic self-consciousness is typical of neo-noir. *Basic Instinct*'s sexual politics also suggest a misogynist theme, as all the major female characters are killers of men: Catherine Tramell's lover Roxy killed her two brothers with a razor, Catherine's friend Hazel Dobkins killed her husband and three children with a knife that she received as a wedding present, and Catherine herself may have killed her parents, her college professor and Johnny Boz. In the film's ambiguous final shot the camera pans down to show us Catherine's personal steel ice pick, as she reaches for it after sex with Nick. Then she releases it. Does this suggest that Catherine is the real killer, but temporarily changes her mind to kill Nick? Alternatively, that the ice pick is a sex toy and part of the film's thematic interweaving of sex and death? As Stephen Cohan puts it, the narrative suggests one thing, namely, that Beth Garner is the killer of Johnny Boz and Gus, while the *mise-en-scène* of the film's ambiguous final shot suggests another, namely, that Catherine is the real (or additional) killer (1998: 269). As Lynda Hart has suggested 'when we ask the film to tell us who *did* it, the only answer it can give us is that *women* did it' (1994: 132). If the erotic thriller, like classic noir, persists in a certain pathologisation of women as criminals, linking sexual agency to criminal propensities, another major cycle of crime films, the female lawyer film, ultimately suggests that a woman's gender is incompatible with her professional identity.

The trial film

If the erotic thriller showed justice as powerless, corrupt or fatally flawed, and impotent to capture sociopathic criminals (*Jagged Edge*), or sexually seductive sirens (*Body Heat*), the trial film or courtroom drama largely responded with a reassuring fantasy of justice restored. Beginning in the 1980s and popularised by the work of Scott Turow (*The Burden of Proof* (1992), *Presumed Innocent* (1990), *Reversible Errors* (2004)) and John Grisham (*The Pelican Brief* (1993), *The Firm* (1993), *The Client* (1994), *A Time to Kill* (1996), *The Chamber* (1996), *The Rainmaker* (1997), *Runaway Jury* (2003)) the literary and cinematic courtroom drama capitalised on public fascination and anxiety about crime and the law. Frequently it presents a narrative conflict between the law and justice, and is resolved by the realignment of the two; for example, a man falsely accused in *Suspect* (1987) or *Presumed Innocent* is ultimately released and the real culprit is discovered or apprehended. The courtroom drama usually features a heroic lawyer who must defend a client wrongfully charged, imprisoned or convicted of a crime for which they are innocent (*Suspect*, *In the Name of the Father*

Fig. 9 The American fantasy of the heroic lawyer: Rudy Baylor (Matt Damon) in
The Rainmaker

(1993)), and who must find out who really committed the crime. In civil law
trial films like *The Rainmaker*, the lawyer usually fights a large bureauc-
racy or corporation on behalf of his or her client, as with Rudy Baylor (Matt
Damon), the underdog lawyer fresh out of law school who fights a corrupt
insurance company who refuse to pay a man who is dying of leukemia.
These films usually point to some problem in the criminal justice system,
whether it be corrupt judges, lawyers or police officers, mistaken or racist
eyewitnesses, inadequate counsel, or negligent corporations putting profit
over people.

Like the mystery story the trial film has a double narrative, with one
story concerned with the discovery of facts and the second with broader
questions of truth and justice that often puts the Law itself on trial.
For example, *Class Action* (1991) is a story about a father and daughter
legal team, Jedidiah (Gene Hackman) and Maggie Ward (Mary Elizabeth
Mastrantonio), who represent opposing sides in a case involving an
automobile manufacturer whose products' petrol tanks explode (a fictionalised version of the Ford Pinto case). The film is also about the ethics
of the legal profession, suggesting that the company's defence attorneys
are corrupt and subvert natural justice by defending the manufacturer's
actions. Sometimes the courtroom drama focuses on the jury process, as
with *Twelve Angry Men* (1957), which stars Henry Fonda as the heroic lone
juror who holds out for a 'not guilty' verdict, and who eventually persuades

his fellow jurors to change their minds, thus suggesting that one person can make a difference. Beginning in the early 1930s, the first period of the courtroom drama was experimental, with what Norman Rosenberg calls 'law noirs', or critical films that did not necessarily show the restoration of justice (1994: 345). In the 1950s and 1960s, the courtroom drama shifted to lawyers as heroic social prophets, battling the forces of unenlightenment, as with Henry Drummond (Spencer Tracy), a thinly-veiled portrait of Clarence Darrow, in *Inherit the Wind* (1960) or Atticus Finch (Gregory Peck) in *To Kill a Mockingbird* (1962). Other examples of the trial film combine a criminal trial with a search for truth in *The Paradine Case* (1947), *Witness for the Prosecution* (1957), *Anatomy of a Murder* (1959) and *Judgment at Nuremberg* (1961).

There were lawyers on American television from its beginnings in the 1940s, including *Famous Jury Trials* (1949–52) and *They Stand Accused* (aka *CrossQuestion* (1949–52)). *Public Prosecutor* (1947–48, revived 1951–52) was the first filmed series for television. With Raymond Burr as the eponymous attorney, *Perry Mason* was perhaps one of the most famous and longest-running legal series and was a model for many later series (for example, *Matlock* (1986–95)). In the 1960s the lawyer became aligned with the social justice issues raised by the Civil Rights movement, and was exemplified in the idealistic attorneys of *The Defenders* (live drama 1957, series 1961–65), *The Trials of O'Brien* (1965–66), *The Lawyers* (aka *The Bold Ones* (1969–72)), *Judd for the Defense* (1967–69), and in the 1970s with *Storefront Lawyers* (1970–71), *The Young Lawyers* (1970–71), *Owen Marshall* (1971–74) and *Petrocelli* (1974–76). After the police officer largely replaced the lawyer as the crusading protagonist in the American crime film in the late 1970s and early 1980s, the lawyer increasingly emerged in primetime television, as in the hit show *LA Law* (1986–94). A number of short-lived shows like *The Trials of Rosie O'Neill* (1990–92), *Sweet Justice* (1994–95) and *Murder One* (1995–97) soon followed, but in the 1990s the top-rated US television shows again included courtroom dramas, among them *Law and Order*, *Ally McBeal* and *The Practice*, and more recently *Boston Legal*, while in the UK, top-rated shows included *Crown Court* (1972–84) and *Rumpole of the Bailey* (play 1975, series 1978–92).

Where television preserves the heroic role of the lawyer as crusader, the trial film of recent decades suggests that justice is profoundly compromised. For example, *The Star Chamber* (1983) tells the story of a secret group of vigilante judges who decide to take the law into their own hands, and who hire a killer to execute those who have escaped justice because of legal 'technicalities'. Where *The Star Chamber* aligned criminality with a corrupt judiciary, *The Juror* (1996) examined the corruption of the jury system, with an eponymous juror (Demi Moore) intimidated by a mobster (Alec Baldwin) into voting him not guilty in a criminal trial. Some trial films are hybrid stories, combining courtroom drama with the thriller, such as *The Firm*, which tells the story of an idealistic young attorney, Mitch McDeere (Tom Cruise), who discovers his prestigious new law firm is really a criminal enterprise of money laundering and extortion, or *The Devil's Advocate* (1997), a horror/courtroom drama in which attorney Kevin Lomax (Keanu Reeves) finds out that his boss John Milton (Al Pacino) is literally the devil. *Primal Fear* (1996) subverts the trial film's basic premise that justice is always restored, in its story of a beatific young man, Aaron Stampler (Edward Norton), who turns out to be a clever sociopath, and who manipulates his lawyer Martin Vail (Richard Gere) into believing that he committed the crime under the influence of an alternate personality. The film ends with Stampler's triumphant revelation of his ruse to Vail, which has unfortunately led to his successful acquittal. If the heroic lawyer film depicts the law as a weapon that can avenge victims and acquit the innocent, the role of the attorney as the criminal's dupe is central to the neo-noir trial film like *Jagged Edge* and *Primal Fear*. In these films, or in ones like *Final Analysis*, where the dupe is a psychiatrist rather than lawyer (but again played by Richard Gere), the criminal manipulates the professional skills and heroic self-image of the lawyer in order to get themselves acquitted.

As Cynthia Lucia's recent study demonstrates, the female lawyer has increasingly come to dominate the trial films of the last three decades, with more than twenty appearing between 1985 and 1995 (2005: 2). Not since the courtroom comedy *Adam's Rib* (1949), with Katharine Hepburn and Spencer Tracy, have female lawyers been seen with such prominence in Hollywood cinema. As Lucia observes, many films in this latest cycle suggest that there is a fundamental incompatibility between being a successful lawyer and being a 'successful woman', with conflicts staged between the female lawyer's personal desires and her professional obligations. Repeatedly, the female lawyer becomes blinded by her inappropriate sexual or emotional desire for her (usually guilty) clients, as we see with Teddy Barnes (Glenn Close) in *Jagged Edge*, Jenny Hudson (Theresa

Russell) in *Physical Evidence*, Thelma Katwuller (Barbara Hershey) in *Defenseless* (1991), and Kathleen Riley (Cher) in *Suspect*, who falls for a juror. There are heroic exceptions such as Darby Shaw (Julia Roberts) in *The Pelican Brief* or Reggie Love (Susan Sarandon) in *The Client*, but by and large the cycle is exemplified by defence attorney Jennifer Haines (Rebecca De Mornay) who falls for her client in *Guilty as Sin* (1993).

Many trial films have a three-part structure, where the trial story brackets a middle section that may be a flashback or investigation into the original crime. The courtroom drama invites the viewer to solve the mystery along with the investigative lawyer for, as with the whodunit, we are in Carol Clover's words 'viewers with a job to do'. Editing and camera techniques often suture the spectator into the story in such a way as to make us feel spatially, and visually, in the jury box, where we too must deliberate on a verdict. Clover suggests that 'the reason that juries are largely unseen in trial movies and the jury system largely uncontested within the regime of cinema is surely that we understand the jury to constitute a kind of necessary blank space in the text, and reserved for occupancy by us' (2000: 253). Like the beginning of *Presumed Innocent*, opening shots of the jury box literally invite us to take our seats, as the diegetic jurors become our narrative surrogates.

If the criminals of neo-noir and the erotic thriller were largely charismatic sexual charmers, and the criminals of the trial film were often corrupt corporations, lawyers or clients, a new type of criminal emerged in the late 1980s, in the serial killer film. In the next chapter we will turn to the enigmatic masterminds and baroque monsters of this kind of film and we will also consider the work of two important postmodern crime auteurs of the last few decades – Quentin Tarantino and David Lynch.

4 THE CRIMINAL II: THE SERIAL KILLER FILM AND POSTMODERN HYBRIDS

The serial killer film

We find the serial killer compelling, not least because of the charismatic chilling performances of gifted actors like Anthony Hopkins as Hannibal Lecter, the cultured cannibal with a taste for music, art and fine cooking in *The Silence of the Lambs*, or Kevin Spacey as John Doe, the spookily clever master planner in *Se7en*. Both compelling and repulsive, the serial killer film repeatedly suggests that these homicidal specialists share certain personality traits: hyper-intelligence, strength, uncanny insight and ubiquity. Catalysed by the Academy Award success of *The Silence of the Lambs*, which won Best Picture, Director, Actor and Actress Oscars in 1992, and which followed earlier entries like *Manhunter* and the low-budget independent *Henry: Portrait of a Serial Killer*, the serial killer film became a prolific and commercially established sub-genre of the crime film by the mid-1990s, where it remains to this day. So popular is the serial killer film that it has migrated to television with a new hybrid crime series, *Dexter* (2006–present), about a forensic technician who is secretly also a serial killer. The serial killer cycle had its roots in much earlier crime cinema, going back to silent era films about Jack the Ripper in *The Lodger* and *Pandora's Box* and key films in the recent contemporary era, which linked serial killing to sexual perversity in *Psycho* and *Peeping Tom* (1960). Many of the first serial killer films in the modern cycle were adaptations of the best-selling crime fiction of Thomas Harris, whose novels *Red Dragon* (1981) and *The Silence of the Lambs* (1988) introduced the character of Hannibal Lecter.

At the same time the trials of notorious real-life killers Ted Bundy (1979) and Henry Lee Lucas (1983) made serial killing prominent news in the US, as did Congressional hearings into serial crime in 1986. One year after the release of *The Silence of the Lambs*, the capture and trial of real-life cannibal Jeffrey Dahmer suggested a further eerie parallel to Thomas Harris's fictional character.

Former FBI agent Robert Ressler has claimed that he coined the term 'serial killer' in the 1970s (replacing the previous term 'stranger killing') through an analogy to film serials. He suggested that film serials, with their traditional cliffhanger endings were based on interruption, frustration and compulsive repetition, and reminded him of the parallel temporal dimension of serial killing, where 'the very act of killing leaves the murderer hanging, because it isn't as perfect as his fantasy. When the Phantom is left sinking in the quicksand, the viewer has to come back next week ... After a murder, the serial murderer thinks of how the crime could have been bettered' (Ressler & Shachtman 1992: 32–34). Like all genre films, which are based on a play of repetition and difference, the serial killer film epitomises the consumption practices of late commodity capitalism. In films like *Copycat*, in which killer Daryll Lee Cullum (Harry Connick Jr) commits crimes modelled on famous earlier serial killer cases, or *Suspect Zero* (2004), in which a serial killer executes other serial killers, this genre self-reflexively foregrounds themes of seriality and repetition, and also subtly echoes the repetition compulsions of both killer and genre consumer. *American Psycho* (2000), based on Bret Easton Ellis's novel (1991), brings together these two elements of compulsive consumerism and repetition compulsion in its satiric story of Patrick Bateman (Christian Bale), a serial-killing Wall Street yuppie. Indeed part of the reason why we are so fascinated by serial killers is because they stand in for what Mark Seltzer calls the 'pathological public sphere', or a culture that celebrates trauma as entertainment and spectacle (1998: 21).

The serial killer also embodies the anonymity and fluidity of population movement enabled by modern society. Colourless and self-effacing, like Hans Beckert in Fritz Lang's *M*, he hides easily in the city; a 'minus man', who nobody suspects to be a killer. Modelled on two serial killers of the time, Peter Kürten, the 'Vampire of Düsseldorf', and Fritz Haarmann, the 'butcher of Hanover', whose respective crimes, trials and subsequent executions received extensive press coverage in the 1920s, *M*'s Beckert (Peter Lorre) is not initially suspected as a child killer because of his cherubic features and unassuming, almost childlike, manner. Like M, which stands for murderer in Lang's eponymous film, the titles of many serial killer films like *Citizen X* (1995) and *The Minus Man* (1999) point to this anonymity as a recurrent element, suggesting that the serial killer presents a crisis of knowledge. As a satire, *The Stepfather* and its sequels (1989, 1992) exaggerates the horror that lurks beneath the mask of societal normality in its story of an ordinary husband and father who periodically slaughters his family, and then moves to a new town to begin again. Not only does the anonymity of the city offer him protection, as does the colourlessness of his personality, the motivation for his compulsion to kill often remains unknowable or inexplicable, even to himself. At the same time these inexplicable repetitive crimes produce intense social anxiety, for we could all be potential victims. To compensate for their intrinsic anonymity, we compulsively try to name and individualise them; tabloids give them pop trademarks like 'The Zodiac Killer' or 'The Night Stalker', or the killers offer up their own signatures such as 'Son of Sam' or 'Jack' or the fictional 'John Doe'. These names connect the serial killer as celebrity author with a method (Jack the Ripper), victim (the Co-ed Killer) or location (The Green River Killer), and many names like the 'Yorkshire Ripper' self-reflexively echo earlier historical killers underscoring the serial, repetitive nature of this form of homicide.

In contrast to this tradition of enigmatic banality is the Grand Guignol monstrosity of Hannibal Lecter in *The Silence of the Lambs*. What Philip L. Simpson calls the neo-Gothic serial killer film reworks archetypal horror, creating the serial killer as a modern version of the monster, vampire, devil, wolf-man, sorcerer, or Jekyll and Hyde personality. The neo-Gothic also romanticises the relationship of killer and victim as a kind of 'dangerous seduction taking place in a haunted landscape of taboo violations and border transgressions' (2000: 25). Let us take a look at these two different traditions in the representation of the serial killer: the neo-Gothic Hannibal Lecter, and the coldly enigmatic John Doe.

The Silence of the Lambs

The Silence of the Lambs is the story of an FBI agent-in-training named Clarice Starling (Jodie Foster), who becomes involved in the investigation of a series of serial killings committed by an unknown assailant nicknamed

Fig. 10 Fascinated by the monster: Dr Frederick Chilton (Anthony Heald) interrogates Hannibal Lecter (Anthony Hopkins) in *The Silence of the Lambs*

'Buffalo Bill' (Ted Levine), because he skins his female victims. Starling is asked by her boss Jack Crawford (Scott Glenn) to interview imprisoned serial killer Hannibal Lecter (Anthony Hopkins), who the FBI believes has information which may help them track down Bill. In return for personal information about her childhood, Lecter drops enigmatic clues about the serial killer to Clarice. With these clues Starling successfully tracks down the killer, who turns out to be a transsexual reconstructing his own body by using his victims' skin. After a chase, Starling kills Buffalo Bill and rescues Catherine Martin (Brooke Smith), who the serial killer has kidnapped and held prisoner in a well in his basement. Meanwhile Hannibal Lecter successfully escapes from prison, and bids farewell to Starling on the phone as he departs to 'have dinner with an old friend' (referring to Dr Chilton, the asylum director he plans to kill).

A blend of the neo-Gothic and investigative realism, *The Silence of the Lambs* was influential in setting the terms of this new cycle in the crime film: the serial killer film. It created several new character types, including the serial killer as a new form of criminal, and a new type of heroic crime investigator who tracks him down: the federal agent, trained in psychological profiling. The figure of Jack Crawford was modelled on the famous FBI profiler and former head of the Behavioural Sciences Unit John Douglas. As a crime procedural, *The Silence of the Lambs* emphasises Starling's and

Crawford's systematic and meticulous search for Buffalo Bill as they criss-cross the country, examining the corpses of Bill's victims, interviewing possible witnesses and trying to profile the killer. Buffalo Bill was a composite of several real killers or serial killers, including Ed Gein who skinned his victims, Edmund Kemper who killed and dismembered his mother and several other women, Ted Bundy who used the cast on his hand as bait to make women get into his van and Gary Heidnik who kept women he kidnapped in a basement pit. Many other serial killer films (and made-for-TV movies) base themselves on real killers and their crimes, such as *The Boston Strangler* (1968) about Albert DeSalvo and *The Stranger Beside Me* (2003) about Ted Bundy. *The Silence of the Lambs'* second serial killer, Hannibal Lecter, embodies the duality of the Romantic villain; like that of Robert Louis Stevenson's famous character the 'Dr Jekyll' half is an educated, urbane and courteous doctor, aesthete and gourmand, yet his 'Hyde' alter-ego kills and eats people. Buffalo Bill remains largely unseen for much of the story, as the narrative concentrates on the intellectual battle that occurs between Lecter and Starling.

Unlike Michael Mann's *Manhunter* in which Lecter (played by Brian Cox in this version) also appears as a character, Jonathan Demme's version of the Lecter story is visually baroque. Clarice must descend into the Gothic dungeons of the mental institution in which Lecter is incarcerated, and which also foreshadow the dungeon-like scenes of Buffalo Bill's basement that we will see later. The editing and *mise-en-scène* emphasise the spectacle of Lecter's incarceration; the elaborate rituals that surround feeding and communication with him; the proscribed items (nothing to be passed other than paper); the method of communication (the loud metal drawer); the mouth restraint and handcuffs, surveillance cameras and guards that surround him. A slow steadicam panning 360 degrees aligns the camera's movement with Clarice's point of view as she meets Barney the nurse and proceeds to walk (alone) down a long corridor past leering patients. Diegetic sound magnifies the clanging of the gates as she approaches Lecter's cell, and the tense atmosphere is heightened by Howard Shore's ominous score. A stylised production design of brown hues and murky lighting intensifies the horror, yet unlike the other inmates, Lecter unexpectedly appears in a pool of light, his blue eyes glittering. Coupled with the quiet intensity of Hopkins' performance, this makes his appearance all the more frightening, because he stands there waiting, as if he already anticipated

Starling's entrance. This uncanny quality of Lecter is emphasised by his pre-ternatural ability to deduce personal details about Clarice, even from faint smells: 'You wear Evian skin cream, and sometimes *L'air du temps* – but not today.'

As a psychological thriller, the film emphasises the psychology of both Lecter and Starling, and the adversarial yet mutually respectful relationship that develops between them. It also complicates the usual formula of the erotic thriller in which the female protagonist is in danger from a male killer. As a trained psychiatrist, Lecter, whose name means 'reader', is an intellec-tual who reads minds as well as books: he is all-seeing and all-knowing; he says to her 'don't lie to me because I will know'. With acute insight, Lecter understands Clarice's ambitious drive to succeed, cuttingly observing:

> You know what you look like to me, with your good bag and your cheap shoes? You look like a rube. A well-scrubbed, hustling rube with a little taste. Good nutrition has given you some length of bone, but you're not more than one generation from poor white trash, are you, Agent Starling? And that accent you've tried so desperately to shed? Pure West Virginia. What's your father, dear? Is he a coal miner? Does he stink of the lamp? You know how quickly the boys found you – all those tedious sticky fumblings in the back seats of cars – while you could only dream of getting out ... getting anywhere ... getting all the way to the FBI.

Lecter gets Clarice to tell him the story of 'the silence of the lambs', a key traumatic moment in her childhood when she tried, but failed, to save a spring lamb from the slaughterhouse. The film's title is also a metaphor for Clarice's subsequent career as a law professional. Unable to save the spring lambs or her police officer father who was murdered when she was a child, Clarice's drive will be finally vindicated with her successful rescue of Buffalo Bill's next intended victim, Catherine Martin.

Lecter's charismatic personality and acute insight is intensified through tight framing which gives us increasingly claustrophobic close-ups of his eyes and face. Because Lecter is imprisoned behind clear Plexiglas rather than prison bars, the space between he and Starling becomes increasingly intimate. Framing and editing bring us closer and closer to Lecter in an exchange of shot/reverse-shots that intensify Clarice's physical proximity and psychological vulnerability. We have already heard from Dr Chilton about Lecter's tremendous power and brutality, as he warns Clarice of the consequences of getting too (physically) close, and we are also reminded of Crawford's earlier warning to Clarice not to let Lecter 'get inside her head'.

Hannibal Lecter's demonic alter-ego suggests a Romantic notion of criminality; that beneath our cultured and civilised surface rage the forces of the id: uncontrollable passions, demonic possessions and folkloric archetypes. This characterisation is evident in the cinematic adaptations of Harris's novels: *Manhunter*, *The Silence of the Lambs*, *Hannibal*, *Red Dragon* (2002) and *Hannibal Rising* (2007). This is also why many serial killers appear in horror movies, and why the two genres overlap, particularly with 1970s and 1980s slasher horror like *Halloween* (1978), *Friday the 13th* (1980) and *A Nightmare on Elm Street* (1984) in which the monsters are serial killers. But where Lecter is a baroque monster who inspires horror, another form of the serial killer creates dread: the cerebral cipher John Doe.

Se7en

Se7en's narrative follows the murderous trail of a killer known only as 'John Doe', who has adopted the Seven Deadly Sins as his homicidal model. Over seven days, seven murders that punish those who are guilty of Gluttony, Greed, Sloth, Lust, Pride, Envy and Wrath are disclosed. Only seven days from retirement, Detective William Somerset (Morgan Freeman) is assigned to investigate this series of crimes, together with his junior partner Detective David Mills (Brad Pitt). After five murders, John Doe unexpectedly turns himself in to the police, promising to reveal the location of his last two victims. He leads the detectives out of the city, to a deserted location where a mail truck appears, delivering what turns out to be the decapitated head of Detective Mills' pregnant wife Tracy (Gwyneth Paltrow), which Doe has previously placed in a box. Doe confesses that he envied Mills' ordinary life, and admits that Tracy's murder was the enactment of his own sin of Envy. The gruesome revelation of Tracy's murder is the culminating act in John Doe's plan, which is to encourage Detective Mills to 'become Wrath' (the final deadly sin), violate his duty as an officer of the law and execute Doe in the film's climax – which Mills subsequently does. Arrested for murder, the film ends with Mills driven away by the police as a saddened Somerset watches.

Combined with an evocative soundtrack (a variant of Nine Inch Nails' 'Closer' track) over the opening credit sequence's scratchy, textured visual design, *Se7en* constructs an atmosphere of dread which builds steadily through its tight narrative structure of seven days and several murders, to its horrifying ending. Using a silver retention process in the film processing, together with a chiaroscuro lighting scheme, cinematographer Darius Khondji created a dark, moody and bleak *mise-en-scène*, where it constantly rains. *Se7en* is a neo-noir detective story set in a city that is no-place, but far from utopian. Art design makes the location purposively anonymous, with no details in the street signs, costumes, police cars or helicopters to identify the city or time. The city is also trapped within an endless temporal loop of repetition in which corruption, violence and sin recur day after day after day, revealing a world of apathy, cynicism and hopelessness. When Somerset questions a particularly bizarre and brutal act of domestic murder, his captain replies, 'it's the way it's always been'. In this way *Se7en* foregrounds social anxieties about urban crime and random violence, but also displaces them onto the mystified figure of the serial killer.

Each of Doe's crimes are brutal in their corporeal specificity: an obese agoraphobic is force-fed to death (Gluttony); a lawyer is forced to cut a pound of flesh from his own body (Greed); a 'drug-dealing pederast' is systematically starved to coma and living-death over a year (Sloth); a prostitute is impaled on a knife-phallus (Lust); a model is mutilated and chooses suicide over disfigurement (Pride); a detective murders an unarmed defendant (Wrath); and Doe himself kills a pregnant woman (Envy). Doe's own murderous practice mutilates and transforms the bodies of his victims (he explodes Gluttony, dissects Greed, starves Sloth, mutilates Pride and punctures Lust). Similarly, his journals reveal his compulsive interest in the body, and more particularly in the grotesque, abnormal, eviscerated or dissected body.

Serial killer John Doe presents us with an interpretative dead end (he has no identity, past, name or fingerprints), which only intensifies his enigmatic power. His library ID card lists his name as 'Jonathan Doe', the traditional nomenclature given to unidentified bodies. He has successfully erased himself from social existence (the police can find no social security number, or any identifying papers) and he has even removed his own fingerprints by slicing the skin off his fingertips. In other words, John Doe's name literalises the dread produced by the anonymity and illegibility of real-life serial killers as the 'abnormal normal' (Seltzer 1998: 7). Referring to his criminal master plan, Doe says to the two detectives: 'I'm not exceptional. This is though ... my work.'

Where the neo-primitivist, apolitical serial killers of *Natural Born Killers* and *Kalifornia* (1993) are apocalyptic, in the restricted sense that their violence is destructive rather than revelatory (Simpson 2000: 181), *Se7en*'s John Doe typifies what Richard Tithecott calls the warrior knight, in that he sees himself as a messianic and punitive agent of God ('I did not choose, I was chosen'), transforming his monstrous actions into prophetic purpose (1997: 150). If we recall that one of the obsolete meanings of the word 'monster' derives from the Latin *monstrum* (which refers to a divine portent or warning in the form of something extraordinary or unnatural), John Doe is a monster because he enacts the apocalypse through his crimes. Somerset is the first to realise that Doe is 'preaching' and that 'this is all about atonement for sin, and the murders are like forced contrition'. Doe adopts the sensational formula of the Seven Deadly Sins as he tells Somerset: 'Wanting people to listen, you can't just tap them on the shoulder anymore. You have to hit them with a sledgehammer, and then you'll notice you have their strict attention.' Doe believes society will 'puzzle over and study and follow his work ... forever', and in this sense, understands his crimes as an artistic and theological allegory that teaches and instructs.

John Doe and Hannibal Lecter were two different kinds of criminal masterminds which built on Gothic and Romantic traditions of monstrosity, as well as earlier literary villains like Sherlock Holmes' arch nemesis Dr Moriarty. In the last three decades other criminal portraits appeared in the work of a range of crime auteurs, from the gangsters of Francis Coppola and Martin Scorsese, to the hit men of Quentin Tarantino and the sexual perverts of David Lynch.

Crime auteurs: Tarantino and Lynch

In *Reservoir Dogs, Pulp Fiction, Jackie Brown* and *Kill Bill vol. 1* (2003) and *Kill Bill vol. 2* (2004), as well as in the screenplay for *True Romance* (1993), Quentin Tarantino's extensive and complex use of pastiche from many different cinematic genres, cycles and traditions reflects his encyclopedic knowledge of film history as a cinephile and former video-store employee, and is one of the strongest arguments for considering him a postmodern crime auteur, or one who uses the devices of *intertextuality* (see Glossary) and pastiche. His films are intertextual dialogues with film history, both citing and recreating the conventions of anime, spaghetti westerns, Hong Kong kung-fu and the films of the Shaw Brothers and Bruce Lee, as well as blaxploitation, the revenge film, Japanese samurai films and many other genres. Tarantino reworks the martial arts revenge story and the western (*Kill Bill*) and the gangster story (*True Romance, Pulp Fiction*). *Reservoir Dogs* is both a homage to the heist film and to Stanley Kubrick's classic *The Killing*, but also an unusual spin on the formula. It is a crime film which focuses on the heist's aftermath, in this case, an unsuccessful robbery of a jewellery store in which some of the team are shot. Divisions appear as the team realises that their failure can only be explained by the fact that one of them must be a traitor and undercover police officer. Alluding to *The Taking of Pelham One Two Three* (1974), we have a story of criminals who are known only through their code-names (Mr Blonde, Mr Pink, Mr Orange, and so forth), and who are brought together by ageing crime boss Joe Cabot (played by classic noir icon Lawrence Tierney) and his son Eddie (Chris Penn). Tarantino's recycling of pop culture, epitomised by the title of his film *Pulp Fiction*, also occurs through his nostalgic musical citations of many 1970s soundtracks, from the theme music to television shows *The Green Hornet* (1966–67) and *Ironside*, to classic Hollywood composers like Bernard Herrmann ('Twisted Nerve') in the soundtrack for *Kill Bill vol. 1*. This postmodern recycling also occurs through his casting practices, as he pays homage to many classic performers from American cinema of the 1970s like Pam Grier, John Travolta and Robert Forster.

Tarantino is known for his thematic and stylistic concern with violence; yet despite the cartoon-like representation of violence typified by the Bride's decapitation and mutilation of her 'Crazy 88' assailants in *Kill Bill vol. 1*, dialogue is almost more significant than action. Tarantino's films are filled with long philosophical digressions, on everything from the difference between American and French fast food ('le Big Mac') discussed by two hit men, Jules (Samuel L. Jackson) and Vincent (John Travolta), in *Pulp Fiction*, to the heist team's long debate over the meaning of Madonna's song 'Like a Virgin' at the beginning of *Reservoir Dogs*. Tarantino's films also feature scrambled narratives which require the viewer to reconstruct what happened in the heist in *Reservoir Dogs*, and the story which comes full circle with a robbery in a diner in *Pulp Fiction*. This latter film has three story lines, and each of them is a homage to different forms of the crime film. The first is the story of two professional hitmen, Vincent and Jules; the second, a story of a boxer, Butch (Bruce Willis), who refuses to take the fall (alluding to many noir boxing classics like *Body and Soul* and *The Set-up*); and the third, a story of two love-bird criminals Pumpkin (Tim Roth) and Honey Bunny (Amanda Plummer) (an entire sub-genre from *Gun Crazy* to *Natural Born Killers*). Tarantino puts the cinema of crime into a cultural blender, reworking narrative formulas into self-reflexive homage and adding his own style of humour.

Where Tarantino creates a stylised portrait of violence and criminality, which largely centres on the world of the professional criminal – the gangster and hitman – David Lynch focuses on the violence and criminality to be found beneath the everyday suburban world. Most characteristically in *Blue Velvet*, and in his television series *Twin Peaks* (1990–91), Lynch's films suggest that there is a world of sexual perversity, violence, incest and sadism beneath the iconic white picket fences that separate each of us from our neighbours. This dichotomy is suggested by the opening sequence of *Blue Velvet* which tracks through and delves into the beautiful green lawns of a peaceful suburb to show us a cacophonous world of murderous insects. The film tells us the story of post-adolescent voyeur Jeffrey Beaumont (Kyle MacLachlan) who one day finds a dismembered ear. This surreal discovery ultimately leads him to a bizarre sexual world, where he meets a beautiful woman, Dorothy Vallens (Isabella Rossellini). Vallens does not turn out to be the manipulative femme fatale we might expect in neo-noir, but rather is a masochistic victim of her insane lover Frank Booth (demonically played by Dennis Hopper).

Similarly, in *Twin Peaks*, Dale Cooper, played by recurring Lynchian actor Kyle MacLachlan is an FBI agent who comes to the small town of Twin Peaks to investigate the slaying of Laura Palmer (Sheryl Lee). Her murderer turns out to be her own father, suggesting here that patriarchy is literally murderous. This hit TV series led to the unsuccessful spin-off film *Twin Peaks: Fire Walk With Me* (1992). Like *Twin Peaks* more recent Lynch films like *Lost Highway*, *Mulholland Dr.* and *Inland Empire* are dominated by dream-like imagery. Lynch's films are postmodern, not because he uses intertextuality and pastiche as principal techniques like Tarantino, but because his work calls into question the very boundaries of what is reality and what is representation. Like Tarantino he manipulates narrative structure and chronology, but unlike Tarantino's stories which allow for a simple reordering by the viewer, Lynch's films problematise the very convention of narrative closure and coherence, and do not necessarily offer the viewer any solutions to his cinematic puzzles. Although much of Lynch's work does not fall into conventional generic categories, and several of his films (*The Elephant Man* (1980), *The Straight Story* (1999)) are not crime films at all, his highly stylised and dream-like stories, enhanced by hypnotic musical scores and strange characters (like 'The Log Lady' and 'The One-Armed Man' in *Twin Peaks*) are waking dreams. For example *Mulholland Dr.* features dual (and mutually contradictory) stories: the first, featuring Diane Selwyn (Naomi Watts) and Camilla (Laura Elena Harring), is a tragic lesbian love story which ends in murder-suicide; the second is a story of fresh-faced actress Betty Elms and amnesiac mystery woman Rita (played again by Watts and Harring), who act as a pair of Nancy Drew-like investigators trying to figure out Rita's true identity. *Mulholland Dr.* transforms Los Angeles into a surreal landscape, and by simultaneously showing us Hollywood as both vicious industry and mythic dreamworld, calls the very nature of its own 'reality' into question. Lynch suggests that the world of crime is never far from the so-called 'normal' world, that reality is like a waking dream and that to assume otherwise is to be delusional. Like the car travelling towards Mulholland Drive, Lynch's films are oneiric journeys that resist any final narrative meaning.

As the postmodern films of Tarantino and Lynch suggest, the crime film continues to evolve, taking ever new forms, while often self-reflexively citing the history of its own representation. New directions and combinations of the crime story, from comic book special effects films to adaptations of graphic novels and computer games show us that the crime film will likely take unforeseen directions in the future, and will continue to hybridise with other genres like science fiction, comedy, romance, war and action films. The continuing popularity of the amateur murder mystery on television shows (with ever-new adaptations of Arthur Conan Doyle and Agatha Christie) and the commercial popularity of shows like *CSI* and *Law and Order* indicate that the public's thirst for solving enigmatic narrative scenarios is far from quenched. Similarly, the rich history of the courtroom drama, the police story and the private eye drama, along with newer developments like the serial killer film, show the continuing aesthetic and commercial popularity of the crime story. Martin Scorsese and Guy Ritchie continue to work in the gangster film, and join other auteurs who have worked in the field of crime, including Sidney Lumet, Alfred Hitchcock, John Singleton, Mike Hodges, John Woo and Brian De Palma. Although crime films remain an overwhelmingly male-dominated field, in terms of stories and directors, like much of the industry worldwide, filmmakers like Kimberly Peirce, Mary Harron and Patty Jenkins offer some hope that more women filmmakers will work in these genres. Although this study has focused on the Anglo-American tradition of the crime film, some of the most exciting recent crime films have been made in South Korea (*Oldboy* (2003), *Lady Vengeance* (2005)), Hong Kong (*Infernal Affairs* (2002)) and Argentina (*The Aura* (2005), demonstrating the rich diversity and global fascination with stories about crime, criminality and violence. With this interest extending internationally, it is highly likely that crime films will continue to be a powerful tradition in film and television.

GLOSSARY

Anthopometry – First proposed by Alphonse Bertillon (1853–1914) in 1879 and adopted by the French police in 1883, this was a system of identification and classification of criminals, designed to track offenders in the criminal justice system. It consisted of eleven detailed measurements of specific parts of a criminal's body, such as the length of the arm bone, the shape of the ear, and so on, together with a series of photographs (including the first mug shots) and systematised descriptions of the offender. Widely adopted by the 1890s but replaced by fingerprinting in the early twentieth century.

Biometrics – Technological means of identification for the purposes of crime prevention, it consists of four principal components: digital fingerprint and handprint scanning, iris/retinal scanning, facial scanning and voiceprint scanning. Increasingly used in the US since 9/11 as a tool of customs and immigration control.

Dactyloscopy – The study of fingerprints. Used for identification and other tasks in law enforcement.

Expressionism – German Art movement beginning in the late 1910s in theatre, and spreading to the visual arts and cinema by the early 1920s, and characterised by highly stylised and artificial *mise-en-scène*, performance, dramatic lighting effects, and oblique camera angles and sets. This visual stylisation often expressed psychological states of mind such as madness.

Film noir – A cycle of largely low-budget crime films from the early 1940s to the late 1950s, and often marked as beginning with the release of *The Maltese Falcon* in 1941 and ending with *Touch of Evil* in 1958. Characterised by a distinctive visual style which included chiaroscuro lighting, canted camera angles and a complex narrative with voice-overs and flashbacks, these films included heist, boxing and private-eye stories, gangster films, police procedurals and narratives centred on a femme fatale, such as *Double Indemnity* (1944) and *The Postman Always Rings Twice* (1946).

Hermeneutics – Originally referred to the principles of interpreting religious writings (specifically the Bible), but since the nineteenth century, and under the influence of German philosophers Friedrich Schleiermacher and Wilhelm Dilthey, refers to the methodologies, theories and procedures of reading and interpreting texts.

Intertextuality – The creation of meaning through the indirect or direct citation of one or more cultural texts, such as a film, play, song or book in another cultural text. For example, Guy Hamilton's *The Mirror Crack'd* is full of cinematic references and self-reflexivity. Through dialogue and imagery it alludes to the famous 'poisoned spoon' in Alfred Hitchcock's *Suspicion*. It also features Elizabeth Taylor and Kim Novak playing fictional movie stars whose roles make fun of their real-life careers.

Pastiche – An attribute of postmodernism (see below, in Postmodern) developed from the work of Fredric Jameson in which the style or attributes of a work of art are copied, but without ironic intent, in what has been described as 'blank parody'.

Physiognomy – Medieval belief, which had its roots in the Greek understanding that the body consisted of fluids called 'humours' which were connected to the four basic elements (fire, earth, water, air) and the seasons, and that an imbalance in the humours affected health and personality. There were four basic personality types: sanguine, choleric, phlegmatic and melancholic, based upon the predominance of a given 'humour' (blood, yellow bile, phlegm and black bile) so, for example, a choleric person had too much yellow bile, and was often quick to anger. Physiognomy assumed that there was an intrinsic relationship between a person's physical appearance, especially the face, and their personality.

Postmodern – Refers to a historical period since the 1940s as well as to a stylistic attribute of postmodernism in architecture, music, literature, art history and film. A difficult concept to define, postmodernism suggests that it marks the historical end of modernism, but other scholars have argued that it is not a separate period, but an extension or outgrowth of modernism. As theorised by Fredric Jameson, Jean Baudrillard and Jean-Francois Lyotard, among other scholars, postmodernism is a theoretical and aesthetic movement which critiques many of modernism's central claims or 'grand narratives', such as the privileging of high art over popular culture, or the belief that we can distinguish between reality and representation. Above all, postmodernism understands the world of late capitalism as characterised by the proliferation of images and representation. Postmodern techniques can include the use of self-reflexivity, pastiche, intertextuality, parody, playfulness and irony, with an emphasis on fractured forms, discontinuous narratives and the decentered and deconstructed subject.

Production Code (Hays/Breen Code) – US System of self-censorship instituted by major Hollywood studios in the classical era, it was first administered by Will Hays (1922) then by Joseph Breen (1934), who developed and adapted it from Hays' original. Under Breen the Production Code Administration (PCA) was formed and the code became rigidly enforced in 1934, routinely forbidding the representation of certain subjects, including explicit sex and violence, miscegenation, the commission of crimes, drug taking and other matters. It was replaced by the Motion Picture Ratings system in 1968.

Volstead Act (1919–33) – US legislation which prohibited the consumption, distribution and sale of alcohol, and which enacted the era commonly referred to as 'Prohibition'.

FILMOGRAPHY

Because the numbers of crime films are extremely large, this is meant to be a selective guide to key British and American crime films, and with a small selection of other international titles.

A note on dates: as theatrical release dates may vary by country, I have selected the copyright date for all British films (which may precede the theatrical release date by one year), and the theatrical release date for all US films.

Absence of Malice (Sydney Pollack, 1981, US)
Absolute Power (Clint Eastwood, 1997, US)
Ace Ventura: Pet Detective (David Pemberton, 1994, US)
A Clockwork Orange (Stanley Kubrick, 1971, UK)
A Cry in the Dark aka *Evil Angels* (Fred Schepisi, 1988, Australia/US)
Accused (Thornton Freeland, 1936, UK)
Accused, The (William Dieterle, 1949, US)
Accused, The (Jonathan Kaplan, 1988, US)
Across 110th Street (Barry Shear, 1972, US)
Adam's Rib (George Cukor, 1949, US)
Adventures of Robin Hood, The (Michael Curtiz and William Keighley, 1938, US)
Adventures of Sherlock Holmes, The (Alfred Werker, 1939, UK)
A Fish Called Wanda (Charles Crichton, 1988, US/UK)
After Dark, My Sweet (James Foley, 1990, US)
After the Thin Man (W. S. Van Dyke, 1936, US)
Against All Odds (Taylor Hackford, 1984, US)
A History of Violence (David Cronenberg, 2005, US)
Aileen: Life and Death of a Serial Killer (Nick Broomfield and Joan Churchill, 2003, UK)

Aileen Wuornos: The Selling of a Serial Killer (Nick Broomfield, 1992, UK)
A Kiss Before Dying (Gerd Oswald, 1955, US)
A Kiss Before Dying (James Dearden, 1991, US)
Al Capone (Richard Wilson, 1959, US)
Alias Jimmy Valentine (Maurice Tourneur, 1915, US)
Alibi (Roland West, 1929, US)
Along Came a Spider (Lee Tamahori, 2001, US)
Alphabet Murders, The (Frank Tashlin, 1965, UK)
Alphaville aka *Une Etrange aventure de Lemmy Caution* (Jean-Luc Godard, 1965, France)
American Gigolo (Paul Schrader, 1980, US)
American History X (Tony Kaye, 1998, US)
American Psycho (Mary Harron, 2000, US)
Anatomy of a Murder (Otto Preminger, 1959, US)
And Then There Were None (René Clair, 1945, US)
Angels With Dirty Faces (Michael Curtiz, 1938, US)
An Innocent Man aka *Hard Rain* (Peter Yates, 1989, US)
Another Thin Man (W. S. Van Dyke, 1939, US)
A Perfect Murder (Andrew Davis, 1998, US)
A Perfect World (Clint Eastwood, 1993, US)
A Place in the Sun (George Stevens, 1951, US)
Appointment With Death (Michael Winner, 1988, US)
A Prize of Arms (Cliff Owen, 1962, UK)
A Rage in Harlem (Bill Duke, 1991, US)
Armored Car Robbery (Richard Fleischer, 1950, US)
A Scanner Darkly (Richard Linklater, 2006, US)
L'Ascenseur pour l'echafaud/Lift to the Scaffold (Louis Malle, 1957, France)
A Simple Plan (Sam Raimi, 1998, US)
A Soldier's Story (Norman Jewison, 1984, US)
Asphalt Jungle (John Huston, 1950, US)
A Time To Kill (Joel Schumacher, 1996, US)
Aura, El/The Aura (Fabián Bielinsky, 2005, Argentina)
Baby Face Nelson (Don Siegel, 1957, US)
Bad Day at Black Rock (John Sturges, 1955, US)
Bad Influence (Curtis Hanson, 1990, US)
Badlands (Terrence Malick, 1973, US)
Bad Lieutenant (Abel Ferrara, 1992, US)
Bad Seed, The (Mervyn LeRoy, 1956, US)
Bad Timing (Nicolas Roeg, 1980, UK)
Bande à part/Band of Outsiders (Jean-Luc Godard, 1964 France)

Bandit Queen (Shekhar Kapur, 1994, India)
Bangville Police (Henry Lehman, 1913, US)
Barton Fink (Joel Coen, 1991, US)
Basic Instinct (Paul Verhoeven, 1992, US)
Basic Instinct 2 (Michael Caton-Jones, 2006, US/UK)
Bête humaine, La /Human Beast (Jean Renoir, 1938, France)
Betrayed (Costa-Gavras, 1988, US)
Beyond a Reasonable Doubt (Fritz Lang, 1956, US)
Beyond a Reasonable Doubt (John Laing, 1980, New Zealand)
Big Caper, The (Robert Stevens,1957, US)
Big Clock, The (John Farrow, 1948, US)
Big Combo, The (Joseph H. Lewis, 1955, US)
Big Heat, The (Fritz Lang, 1953, US)
Big House, The (George W. Hill, 1930, US)
Big Lebowski, The (Joel Coen, 1998, US)
Big Sleep, The (Howard Hawks, 1946, US)
Birds, The (Alfred Hitchcock, 1963,US)
Bitter Moon (Roman Polanski, 1992, US)
Blackboard Jungle (Richard Brooks, 1955, US)
Black Dahlia, The (Brian De Palma, 2006, US)
Blackmail (Alfred Hitchcock, 1929, UK)
Black Marble, The (Harold Becker, 1980, US)
Blackout, The (Abel Ferrara, 1997, US)
Black Widow (Bob Rafelson, 1987, US)
Blade Runner (Ridley Scott, 1982, US)
Blessures assassines, Les/Murderous Maids (Jean-Pierre Denis, 2000, France)
Blood Simple (Joel Coen, 1984, US)
Blood Work (Clint Eastwood, 2002, US)
Bloody Mama (Roger Corman, 1970, US)
Blow Out (Brian De Palma, 1981, US)
Blow-up (Michelangelo Antonioni, 1966, UK)
Blue Dahlia, The (George Marshall, 1946, US)
Blue Lamp, The (Basil Dearden, 1949, UK)
Blue Steel (Kathryn Bigelow, 1990, US)
Blue Velvet (David Lynch, 1986, US)
Bob le flambeur (Jean-Pierre Melville, 1955, France)
Body and Soul (Robert Rossen, 1947, US)
Body Double (Brian De Palma, 1984, US)
Body Heat (Lawrence Kasdan, 1981, US)
Body of Evidence (Uli Edel, 1992, US)

Boksuneun naui geot/Sympathy for Mr Vengeance (Chan-Wook Park, South Korea, 2002)

Bone Collector, The (Phillip Noyce, 1999, US)

Bonnie and Clyde (Arthur Penn, 1967, US)

Bonnie Parker Story, The (William Witney, 1958, US)

Born to Kill (Robert Wise, 1947, US)

Boston Strangler, The (Richard Fleischer, 1968, US)

Boucher, Le/The Butcher (Claude Chabrol, 1970, France)

Bound (Andy and Larry Wachowski, 1996, US)

Bowling for Columbine (Michael Moore, 2002, US)

Boys Don't Cry (Kimberly Pierce, 1999, US)

Boyz N The Hood (John Singleton, 1991, US)

Brandon Teena Story, The (Susan Muska and Gréta Olafsdóttir, 1997, US)

Brasher Doubloon, The (John Brahm, 1947, US)

Breakdown (Jonathan Mostow, 1997, US)

Brick (Rian Johnson, 2005, US)

Brighton Rock (John Boulting, 1947, UK)

Brother (Takeshi Kitano, 2000, Japan)

Brotherhood, The (Martin Ritt, 1968, US)

Brute Force (Jules Dassin, 1947, US)

Büchse der Pandora, Die/Pandora's Box (G. W. Pabst, 1929, Germany)

Bullets or Ballots (William Keighley, 1936, US)

Bullitt (Peter Yates, 1968, US)

Burden of Proof, The (Mike Robe, 1992, TV, US)

Burning Bed (Robert Greenwald, 1984, TV, US)

Cabinet des Dr Caligari, Das/The Cabinet of Dr Caligari (Robert Weine, 1919, Germany)

Caché/Hidden (Michael Haneke, 2005, France)

Caged Heat (Jonathan Demme, 1974, US)

Call Northside 777 (Henry Hathaway, 1948, US)

Cape Fear (J. Lee Thompson, 1962, US)

Cape Fear (Martin Scorsese, 1991, US)

Captive City, The (Robert Wise, 1952, US)

Capturing the Friedmans (Andrew Jarecki, 2003, US)

Carlito's Way (Brian De Palma, 1993, US)

Casino (Martin Scorsese, 1995, US)

Cat and the Canary, The (Paul Leni, 1927, US)

Catch Me If You Can (Steven Spielberg, 2002, US)

Cell, The (Tarsem Singh, 2000, US)

Cellular (David R. Ellis, 2004, US)

Cercle rouge, Le/Red Circle (Jean-Pierre Melville, 1970, France)
Chamber, The (James Foley, 1996, US)
Chandler (Paul Magwood, 1971, US)
Charley Varrick (Don Siegel, 1973, US)
Charlie's Angels (McG, 2000, US)
Charlie's Angels 2: Full Throttle (McG, 2003, US)
China Moon (John Bailey, 1994, US)
Chinatown (Roman Polanski, 1974, US)
Chinjeolhan geumjassi/Sympathy for Lady Vengeance (Chan-Wook Park, South
    Korea, 2005)
Choirboys, The (Robert Aldrich,1977, US)
Cidade de Deus/City of God (Kátia Lund and Fernando Mereilles, 2002, Brazil)
Circus (Rob Walker, 2000, UK)
Citizen X (Chris Gerolmo, 1995, TV, US)
Class Action (Michael Apted, 1991, US)
Cleopatra Jones (Jack Starrett, 1973, US)
Cleopatra Jones and the Casino of Gold (Chuck Bail, 1975, US)
Client, The (Joel Schumacher, 1994, US)
Clockers (Spike Lee, 1995, US)
Clue (Jonathan Lynn, 1985, US)
Coffy (Jack Hill, 1973, US)
Collateral (Michael Mann, 2004, US)
Collector, The (William Wyler, 1965, US)
Colors (Dennis Hopper, 1988, US)
Compulsion (Richard Fleischer, 1959, US)
Coogan's Bluff (Don Siegel, 1968, US)
Cool Hand Luke (Stuart Rosenberg, 1967, US)
Consenting Adults (Alan J. Pakula, 1992, US)
Conversation, The (Francis Ford Coppola, 1974, US)
Cook, The Thief, His Wife & Her Lover, The (Peter Greenaway, 1989, UK)
Cop (James B. Harris, 1988, US)
Copland (James Mangold, 1997, US)
Cops (Buster Keaton and Edward F. Cline, 1922, US)
Copycat (Jon Amiel, 1995, US)
Cornered (Edward Dmytryk, 1945, US)
Cotton Club, The (Francis Ford Coppola, 1984, US)
Cotton Comes to Harlem (Ossie Davis, 1970, US)
Crash (Paul Haggis, 2004, US)
Crime and Punishment (Josef von Sternberg, 1935, US)
Crimes and Misdemeanors (Woody Allen, 1989, US)

Criminal, The (Joseph Losey, 1960, UK)
Criminal, The (Julian Simpson, 1999, UK)
Criminal Code, The (Howard Hawks, 1931, US)
Criss Cross (Robert Siodmak, 1949, US)
Crossfire (Edward Dmytryk, 1947, US)
Croupier (Mike Hodges, 1997, UK/Ireland)
Crown v. Stevens (Michael Powell, 1936, UK)
Cruising (William Friedkin, 1980, US)
Curse of the Jade Scorpion, The (Woody Allen, 2001, US)
Cutter's Way (Ivan Passer, 1981, US)
Damned Don't Cry, The (Vincent Sherman, 1950, US)
Dance With a Stranger (Mike Newell, 1984, UK)
Dark City (Alex Proyas, 1997, US)
Dark Mirror, The (Robert Siodmak, 1946, US)
Dark Passage (Delmer Daves, 1947, US)
Da Vinci Code, The (Ron Howard, 2006, US)
Dead Again (Kenneth Branagh, 1991, US)
Dead Calm (Phillip Noyce, 1989, Australia)
Dead End aka *Cradle of Crime* (William Wyler, 1937, US)
Deadfall (Bryan Forbes, 1967, UK)
Dead Man Walking (Tim Robbins, 1995, US)
Dead of Night (Alberto Cavalcanti, 1945, UK)
Dead Pool, The (Buddy Van Horn, 1988, US)
Dead Presidents (Allen and Albert Hughes, 1995, US)
Dead Reckoning (John Cromwell, 1947, US)
Death on The Nile (John Guillermin, 1978, UK)
Death Wish (Michael Winner, 1974, US)
Deceived (Damian Harris, 1991, US)
Deep Cover (Bill Duke, 1992, US)
Defenseless (Martin Campbell, 1991, US)
Déjà Vu (Tony Scott, 2006, US)
Deliverance (John Boorman, 1972, US)
Departed, The (Martin Scorsese, 2006, US)
Desperate Hours, The (William Wyler, 1955, US)
Detective, The (Gordon Douglas, 1968, US)
Detective Story (William Wyler, 1951, US)
Detour (Edgar Ulmer, 1945, US)
Devil in a Blue Dress (Carl Franklin, 1995, US)
Devil's Advocate, The (Taylor Hackford, 1997, US)
Diabolique (Jeremiah S. Chechik, 1996, US)

Diaboliques, Les/The Fiends (Henri-Georges Clouzot, 1955, France)
Dial M For Murder (Alfred Hitchcock, 1954, US)
Dillinger (Max Nosseck, 1945, US)
Dillinger (John Milius, 1973, US)
Dip hyut shueng hung/The Killer (John Woo, 1989, Hong Kong)
Dirty Harry (Don Siegel, 1971, US)
Disclosure (Barry Levinson, 1994, US)
D.O.A (Rudolph Mate, 1950, US)
Dr Mabuse der Spieler/Dr Mabuse the Gambler (Fritz Lang, 1922, Germany)
Dog Day Afternoon (Sidney Lumet, 1975, US)
Dolores Claiborne (Taylor Hackford, 1995, US)
Domino (Tony Scott, 2005, US)
Donnie Brasco (Mike Newell, 1997, US)
Doorway to Hell (Archie Mayo, 1930, US)
Do The Right Thing (Spike Lee, 1989, US)
Double Indemnity (Billy Wilder, 1944, US)
Double Jeopardy (Bruce Beresford, 1999, US)
Doulos, Le/The Finger Man (Jean-Pierre Melville, 1962, France)
Dragnet (Jack Webb, 1954, US)
Dressed to Kill (Roy William Neill, 1946, US)
Dressed to Kill (Brian De Palma, 1980, US)
Drowning Pool, The (Stuart Rosenberg, 1975, US)
Each Dawn I Die (William Keighley, 1939, US)
East of Eden (Elia Kazan, 1955, US)
Enforcer, The (Bretaigne Windust and Raoul Walsh (uncredited), 1951, US)
Enforcer, The (James Fargo, 1976, US)
Enough (Michael Apted, 2002, US)
Erin Brockovich (Steven Soderbergh, 2000, US)
Escape From Alcatraz (Don Siegel, 1979, US)
Evil Under the Sun (Guy Hamilton, 1981, UK)
Ex-Convict, The (Edwin Porter, 1904, US)
Eye for an Eye (John Schlesinger, 1996, US)
Eye of the Storm (Yuri Zeltser, 1991, US)
Eyes of Laura Mars (Irvin Kershner, 1978, US)
Eyes Wide Shut (Stanley Kubrick, 1999, US)
Face (Antonia Bird, 1997, UK)
Face/Off (John Woo, 1997, US)
Fallen Idol, The (Carol Reed, 1948, UK)
Family Plot (Alfred Hitchcock, 1976, US)
Fantômas (Louis Feuillade, 1913–1914, France)

Farewell My Lovely (Dick Richards, 1975, US/UK)
Fargo (Joel Coen, 1995, US)
Fatal Attraction (Adrian Lyne, 1987, US)
Fatal Beauty (Tom Holland, 1987, US)
Fatal Instinct (Carl Reiner, 1993, US)
FBI Story, The (Mervyn LeRoy, 1959, US)
Fear (James Foley, 1996, US)
Fear City (Abel Ferrara, 1984, US)
Femme Fatale (Brian De Palma, 2002, France)
Femme Nikita, La aka *Nikita* (Luc Besson, 1990, France/Italy)
Fight Club (David Fincher, 1999, US)
File on Thelma Jordan, The (Robert Siodmak, 1949, US)
Final Analysis (Phil Joanou, 1992, US)
Firm, The (Sydney Pollack, 1993, US)
Fletch (Michael Ritchie, 1985, US)
Flic, Un/Cop (Jean-Pierre Melville, 1972, France)
Force of Evil (Abraham Polonsky, 1948, US)
Fort Apache, The Bronx (Daniel Petrie, 1981, US)
Foxy Brown (Jack Hill, 1974, US)
Frantic (Roman Polanski, 1988, US)
French Connection, The (William Friedkin, 1971, US)
French Connection II, The (John Frankenheimer, 1975, US)
Frenzy (Alfred Hitchcock, 1972, UK)
Freudlose Gasse, Die/Joyless Street (G. W. Pabst, 1925, Germany)
Frightened City, The (John Lemont, 1961, UK)
Fugitive, The (Andrew Davis, 1993, US)
Funny Games (Michael Haneke, 1997, Austria)
Fury (Fritz Lang, 1936, US)
Fuzz (Richard A. Colla, 1972, US)
Gambit (Ronald Neame, 1966, UK)
Gangs of New York (Martin Scorsese, 2002, US)
Gangster No. 1 (Paul McGuigan, 2000, UK)
Gaslight aka *Angel Street* (Thorold Dickinson, 1940, UK)
Gaslight (George Cukor, 1944, US)
Gauntlet, The (Clint Eastwood, 1977, US)
George Raft Story, The (Joseph Newman, 1961, US)
Getaway, The (Sam Peckinpah, 1972, US)
Getaway, The (Roger Donaldson, 1994, US)
Get Carter (Mike Hodges, 1970, UK)
Get Shorty (Barry Sonnenfeld, 1995, US)

Ghost Dog: The Way of the Samurai (Jim Jarmusch, 1999, US/France)
Gilda (Charles Vidor, 1946, US)
Gingerbread Man, The (Robert Altman, 1998, US)
Girl Hunters, The (Roy Rowland, 1963, UK)
Glass Key, The (Stuart Heisler, 1942, US)
Glass Shield, The (Charles Burnett, 1994, US)
G Men (William Keighley, 1935, US)
Godfather, The (Francis Ford Coppola, 1972, US)
Godfather Part II, The (Francis Ford Coppola, 1974, US)
Godfather Part III, The (Francis Ford Coppola, 1990, US)
Good Die Young, The (Lewis Gilbert, 1954, UK)
Goodfellas (Martin Scorsese, 1990, US)
Good Son, The (Joseph Ruben, 1993, US)
Gosford Park (Robert Altman, 2001, UK)
Great Gambini, The (Charles Vidor, 1937, US)
Great Mouse Detective, The (Ron Clements, Burny Mattinson, Dave Michener and John Musker, 1986, US)
Great Train Robbery, The (Edwin Porter, 1903, US)
Greed (Erich Von Stroheim, 1924, US)
Green Cockatoo, The aka *Four Dark Hours* (William Cameron Menzies, 1940, UK)
Green Mile, The (Frank Darabont, 1999, US)
Grifters, The (Stephen Frears, 1990, US)
Guilty as Sin (Sidney Lumet, 1993, US)
Gun Crazy (Joseph H. Lewis, 1949, US)
Haine, La/Hate (Mathieu Kassovitz, 1995, France)
Hand that Rocks the Cradle, The (Curtis Hanson, 1992, US)
Hangover Square (John Brahm, 1945, US)
Hannibal (Ridley Scott, 2001, UK/US)
Hannibal Rising (Peter Webber, 2007, US)
Hard Men (J. K. Amalou, 1996, UK)
Harper (Jack Smight, 1966, US)
Heat (Michael Mann, 1995, US)
Heavenly Creatures (Peter Jackson, 1994, New Zealand)
Heist, The (Kurt Voss, 1999, US)
Hell is a City (Val Guest, 1959, UK)
Henry: Portrait of a Serial Killer (John McNaughton, 1986, US)
He Walked By Night (Alfred Werker, 1948, US)
He Who Rides a Tiger (Charles Crichton, 1965, UK)
High Sierra (Raoul Walsh, 1941, US)
History of a Crime (Ferdinand Zecca, 1901, France)

Hit, The (Stephen Frears, 1984, UK)
Hitch-hiker, The (Ida Lupino, 1953, US)
Hollywoodland (Allen Coulter, 2006, US)
Homicide (David Mamet, 1991, US)
Honest (David A. Stewart, 2000, UK)
Honeymoon Killers, The (Leonard Kastle, 1970, US)
Hound of the Baskervilles, The (Sidney Lanfield, 1939, US)
Hound of the Baskervilles, The (Terence Fisher, 1958, UK)
House of Fear, The (Roy William Neill, 1945, US)
How to Steal a Million (William Wyler, 1966, US)
I Am A Fugitive From a Chain Gang (Mervyn LeRoy, 1932, US)
I Confess (Alfred Hitchcock, 1953, US)
Identity (James Mangold, 2003, US)
I'll Sleep When I'm Dead (Mike Hodges, 2003, UK)
Illusionist, The (Neil Burger, 2006, US)
Impulse (Sondra Locke, 1990, US)
In a Lonely Place (Nicolas Ray, 1950, US)
In Cold Blood (Richard Brooks, 1967, US)
In Dreams (Neil Jordan, 1999, US)
Infamous (Douglas McGrath, 2005, US)
Inherit the Wind (Stanley Kramer, 1960, US)
Inside of the White Slave Traffic, The (Frank Beal, 1913, US)
Internal Affairs (Mike Figgis, 1989, US)
In The Cut (Jane Campion, 2003, US/Australia)
In the Heat of the Night (Norman Jewison, 1967, US)
In the Line of Fire (Wolfgang Petersen, 1993, US)
In the Name of the Father (Jim Sheridan, 1993, UK/Ireland)
Intruder in the Dust (Clarence Brown, 1949, US)
I, Robot (Alex Proyas, 2004, US)
Italian Job, The (Peter Collinson, 1969, UK)
Italian Job, The (F. Gary Gray, 2003, US)
I Want to Live! (Robert Wise, 1958, US)
Jackie Brown (Quentin Tarantino, 1997, US)
Jade (William Friedkin, 1995, US)
Jagged Edge (Richard Marquand, 1985, US)
Jennifer 8 (Bruce Robinson, 1992, US)
Joe Macbeth (Ken Hughes, 1955, UK)
Judex (Louis Feuillade, 1916–1917, France)
Judgment at Nuremberg (Stanley Kramer, 1961, US)
Juice (Ernest R. Dickerson, 1992, US)

Juror, The (Brian Gibson, 1996, US)
Kalifornia (Dominic Sena, 1993, US)
Kansas City Confidential (Phil Karlson, 1952, US)
Kennel Murder Case, The (Michael Curtiz, 1933, US)
Key Largo (John Huston, 1948, US)
Kid Galahad (Michael Curtiz, 1937, US)
Kill Bill vol 1. (Quentin Tarantino, 2003, US)
Kill Bill vol 2. (Quentin Tarantino, 2004, US)
Killer Inside Me, The (Burt Kennedy, 1976, US)
Killers, The (Robert Siodmak, 1946, US)
Killers, The (Don Siegel, 1964, US)
Killer's Kiss (Stanley Kubrick, 1955, US)
Killing, The (Stanley Kubrick, 1956, US)
Kill Me Again (John Dahl, 1989, US)
Kill Off, The (Maggie Greenwald,1989, US)
Kind Hearts and Coronets (Robert Hamer, 1949, UK)
King of New York (Abel Ferrara, 1990, US)
Kiss Me Deadly (Robert Aldrich, 1955, US)
Kiss of Death (Henry Hathaway, 1947, US)
Kiss the Girls (Gary Fleder, 1997, US)
Kiss Tomorrow Goodbye (Gordon Douglas, 1950, US)
Kleptomaniac, The (Edwin S. Porter, 1905, US)
Klute (Alan J. Pakula, 1971, US)
Knock On Any Door (Nicholas Ray, 1949, US)
Krays, The (Peter Medak, 1990, UK)
L.A. Confidential (Curtis Hanson, 1997, US)
Ladri di biciclette/The Bicycle Thief (Vittorio De Sica, 1947, Italy)
Lady from Shanghai (Orson Welles, 1947, US)
Lady In a Cage (Walter Grauman, 1964, US)
Lady in Cement (Gordon Douglas, 1968, US)
Lady in the Lake (Robert Montgomery, 1947, US)
Ladykillers, The (Alexander Mackendrick, 1955, UK)
Ladykillers, The (Joel and Ethan Coen, 2004, US)
Lady Vanishes, The (Alfred Hitchcock, 1938, UK)
Lashou Shentan/Hard-Boiled (John Woo, 1992, Hong Kong)
Last Dance (Bruce Beresford, 1996, US)
Last of Sheila, The (Herbert Ross, 1973, US)
Last Seduction, The (John Dahl, 1994, US)
Laughing Policeman, The (Stuart Rosenberg, 1973, US)
Laura (Otto Preminger, 1944, US)

Lavender Hill Mob, The (Charles Crichton, 1951, UK)
Layer Cake (Matthew Vaughn, 2004, UK)
Léon (Luc Besson, 1994, France)
Let 'Em Have it (Sam Wood, 1935, US)
Lethal Weapon (Richard Donner, 1987, US)
Let Him Have It (Peter Medak, 1991, UK)
Letter, The (William Wyler, 1940, US)
Light Sleeper (Paul Schrader, 1992, US)
Lights of New York (Bryan Foy, 1928, US)
Limey, The (Steven Soderbergh, 1999, US)
Lipstick (Lamont Johnson, 1976, US)
List of Adrian Messenger, The (John Huston, 1963, US)
Little Caesar (Mervyn LeRoy, 1930, US)
Little Odessa (James Gray, 1994, US)
Lock, Stock and Two Smoking Barrels (Guy Ritchie, 1998, UK)
Lodger, The (Alfred Hitchcock, 1926, UK)
Long Arm, The (Charles Frend, 1956, UK)
Long Goodbye, The (Robert Altman, 1973, US)
Long Good Friday, The (John MacKenzie, 1979, UK)
Long Kiss Goodnight, The (Renny Harlin, 1996, US)
Long Memory, The (Robert Hamer, 1952, UK)
Looking for Mr. Goodbar (Richard Brooks, 1977, US)
Lost Highway (David Lynch, 1997, US)
Love Crimes (Lizzie Borden, 1992, US)
Love, Honour and Obey (Dominic Anciano and Ray Burdis, 1999, UK)
Lucky Number Slevin (Paul McGuigan, 2006, US)
Lying Lips (Oscar Micheaux, 1939, US)
M (Fritz Lang, 1931, Germany)
Machine Gun Kelly (Roger Corman, 1958, US)
Madigan (Don Siegel, 1968, US)
Magnum Force (Ted Post, 1973, US)
Malice (Harold Becker, 1993, US)
Malice Aforethought (David Blair, 2005, UK)
Maltese Falcon, The (Roy Del Ruth, 1931, US)
Maltese Falcon, The (John Huston, 1941, US)
Manhattan Melodrama (W. S. Van Dyke, 1934, US)
Manhattan Murder Mystery (Woody Allen, 1993, US)
Manhunter (Michael Mann, 1986, US)
Man Who Knew Too Much, The (Alfred Hitchcock, 1934, UK)
Man Who Knew Too Much, The (Alfred Hitchcock, 1955, US)

Man Who Wasn't There, The (Joel Coen, 2001, US)
Mariachi, El (Robert Rodriguez, 1992, US)
Marked Woman (Lloyd Bacon, 1937, US)
Marlowe (Paul Bogart, 1969, US)
Marnie (Alfred Hitchcock, 1964, US)
Mask of Dimitrios, The (Jean Negulesco, 1944, US)
Mask of Fu Manchu, The (Charles Brabin and (uncredited)Charles Vidor, 1932, US)
Masquerade (Bob Swaim, 1988, US)
Match Point (Woody Allen, 2005, US/UK/Luxembourg)
Mean Streets (Martin Scorsese, 1973, US)
Member of the Jury (Bernard Mainwaring, 1937, UK)
Memento (Christopher Nolan, 2000, US)
Menace II Society (Allen and Albert Hughes, 1993, US)
Miami Blues (George Armitage, 1989, US)
Miami Vice (Michael Mann, 2006, US)
Midnight Express (Alan Parker, 1978, US)
Mildred Pierce (Michael Curtiz, 1945, US)
Miller's Crossing (Joel Coen, 1990, US)
Mind of Mr Reeder, The (Jack Raymond, 1939, UK)
Ministry of Fear, The (Fritz Lang, 1944, US)
Minority Report (Steven Spielberg, 2002, US)
Minus Man, The (Hampton Fancher, 1999, US)
Miracles for Sale (Tod Browning, 1939, US)
Mirror Crack'd, The (Guy Hamilton, 1980, UK)
Miss Congeniality (Donald Petrie, 2000, US)
Miss Congeniality 2: Armed and Fabulous (John Pasquin, 2005, US)
Mississippi Burning (Alan Parker, 1988, US)
Mr Moto in Danger Island (Herbert I. Leeds, 1939, US)
Mr Moto's Gamble (James Tinling, 1938, US)
Mr Moto's Last Warning (Norman Foster, 1939, US)
Mr Moto Takes a Vacation (Norman Foster, 1939, US)
Mob, The (Robert Parrish, 1951, US)
Mona Lisa (Neil Jordan, 1986, UK)
Monogrammed Cigarette, The (Harry C. Matthews, 1910, Yankee serial, US)
Monsieur Verdoux (Charles Chaplin, 1947, US)
Monster (Patty Jenkins, 2003, US)
Morning After, The (Sidney Lumet, 1986, US)
Mortal Thoughts (Alan Rudolph, 1991, US)
Mou gaan dou/Infernal Affairs (Wai Keung Lau and Siu Fai Mak, 2002, Hong

Kong)

Ms. 45 (Abel Ferrara, 1981, US)

Mulholland Dr. (David Lynch, 2001, US)

Mulholland Falls (Lee Tamahori, 1996, US)

Murder! (Alfred Hitchcock, 1930, UK)

Murder Ahoy (George Pollock, 1964, UK)

Murder at 1600 (Dwight Little, 1997, US)

Murder at the Gallop (George Pollock, 1963, UK)

Murder at the Vicarage (Julian Amyes, 1986, TV, UK)

Murder by Death (Robert Moore, 1976, US)

Murder by Numbers (Barbet Schroeder, 2002, US)

Murder in the First (Marc Rocco, 1995, US)

Murder Most Foul (George Pollock, 1964, UK)

Murder, My Sweet aka *Farewell my Lovely* (Edward Dmytryk, 1944, US)

Murder on the Orient Express (Sidney Lumet, 1974, UK)

Murder Over New York (Harry Lachman, 1940, US)

Murder She Said (George Pollock, 1961, UK)

Murders in the Rue Morgue, The (Robert Florey, 1932, US)

Murder Will Out (John Gilling, 1952, UK)

Musketeers of Pig Alley (D.W. Griffith, 1912, US)

Music Box (Costa-Gavras, 1989, US)

Mysterious Dr Fu Manchu, The (Rowland V. Lee, 1929, US)

Mysterious Wu Chung Foo (Dir. unknown,1914, Feature Photoplay, US)

Mystery of Dr Fu-Manchu, The (A.E. Coleby, 1923, UK)

Mystic River (Clint Eastwood, 2003, US)

Naked City, The (Jules Dassin, 1948, US)

Name of the Rose, The (Jean-Jacques Annaud, 1986, US)

Narrow Margin, The (Richard Fleischer, 1952, US)

Natural Born Killers (Oliver Stone, 1994, US)

Ned Kelly (Gregor Jordan, 2003, Australia)

Never Let Go (John Guillermin, 1960, UK)

New Jack City (Mario Van Peebles, 1991, US)

Night and the City (Jules Dassin, 1950, UK)

Night and the City (Irwin Winkler, 1992, US)

Night Falls on Manhattan (Sidney Lumet, 1996, US)

Night Moves (Arthur Penn, 1975, US)

Night of the Hunter (Charles Laughton, 1955, US)

No Country for Old Men (Joel Coen, 2007, US)

No Orchids for Miss Blandish (St. John L. Clowes, 1948, UK)

Noose (Edmond T. Greville, 1948, UK)

North by Northwest (Alfred Hitchcock, 1959, US)
North Country (Niki Caro, 2005, US)
Notorious (Alfred Hitchcock, 1946, US)
Nouvelle mission de Judex, La/New Mission of Judex, The (Louis Feuillade, 1917, France)
No Way Out (Roger Donaldson, 1987, US)
Obsession (Brian De Palma, 1976, US)
Ocean's Eleven (Lewis Milestone, 1960, US)
Ocean's Eleven (Steven Soderbergh, 2001, US)
Ocean's Twelve (Steven Soderbergh, 2004, US)
Ocean's Thirteen (Steven Soderbergh, 2007, US)
October Man, The (Roy Ward Baker, 1947, UK)
Odds Against Tomorrow (Robert Wise, 1959, US)
Oldboy (Chan-wook Park, 2003, Korea)
Olvidados, Los/The Young and the Damned (Luis Buñuel, 1950, Mexico)
Once Upon a Time in America (Sergio Leone, 1984, US)
On Dangerous Ground (Nicholas Ray, 1952, US)
One False Move (Carl Franklin, 1992, US)
One Good Cop (Heywood Gould, 1991, US)
Onion Field, The (Harold Becker, 1979, US)
On The Waterfront (Elia Kazan, 1954, US)
Ordeal By Innocence (Desmond Davis, 1984, UK)
Original Gangstas (Larry Cohen, 1996, US)
Ossessione (Luchino Visconti, 1943, Italy)
Out of Sight (Steven Soderbergh, 1998, US)
Out of the Past (Jacques Tourneur, 1947, US)
Pacific Heights (John Schlesinger, 1990, US)
Palmetto (Volker Schlöndorff, 1998, US)
Papillon (Franklin J. Schaffner, 1973, US)
Paradine Case, The (Alfred Hitchcock, 1947, US)
Parallax View, The (Alan J. Pakula, 1974, US)
Patty Hearst (Paul Schrader, 1988, US)
Payroll (Sidney Hayers, 1961, UK)
Pearl of Death, The (Roy William Neill, 1944, US)
Peeping Tom (Michael Powell, 1960, UK)
Pelican Brief, The (Alan J. Pakula, 1993, US)
Performance (Donald Cammell and Nicolas Roeg, 1970, UK)
Perfume: The Story of a Murderer (Tom Tykwer, 2006, US)
Petrified Forest, The (Archie L. Mayo, 1936, US)
Phenix City Story, The (Phil Karlson, 1955, US)

Phone Booth (Joel Schumacher, 2002, US)
Physical Evidence (Michael Crichton, 1989, US)
Piccadilly (E. A. Dupont, 1929, UK)
Piccadilly Third Stop (Wolf Rilla, 1960, UK)
Pickpocket (Robert Bresson, 1959, France)
Pickup on South Street (Samuel Fuller, 1953, US)
Piedone lo sbirro/Flatfoot (Steno, 1973, Italy)
Player, The (Robert Altman, 1992, US)
Play Misty for Me (Clint Eastwood, 1971, US)
Plein Soleil aka *Purple Noon* (René Clément, 1960, France/Italy)
Point Blank (John Boorman, 1967, US)
Point of No Return aka The Assassin (John Badham, 1993, US)
Poison Ivy (Katt Shea, 1992, US)
Portrait in Black (Michael Gordon, 1960, US)
Positive ID (Andy Anderson, 1987, US)
Postman Always Rings Twice, The (Tay Garnett, 1946, US)
Postman Always Rings Twice, The (Bob Rafelson, 1981, US)
Prestige, The (Christopher Nolan, 2006, US)
Presumed Innocent (Alan J. Pakula, 1990, US)
Pretty Boy Floyd (Herbert Leder, 1960, US)
Prick Up Your Ears (Stephen Frears, 1987, UK)
Primal Fear (Gregory Hoblit, 1996, US)
Prince of the City (Sidney Lumet, 1981, US)
Prizzi's Honor (John Huston, 1985, US)
Psycho (Alfred Hitchcock, 1960, US)
Public Enemy, The (William Wellman, 1931, US)
Public Prosecutor, The (Dennis Vance, 1953, UK)
Pulp Fiction (Quentin Tarantino, 1994, US)
Pursuit to Algiers (Roy William Neill, 1945, US)
Q & A (Sidney Lumet, 1990, US)
Racket, The (Lewis Milestone, 1928, US)
Racket, The (John Cromwell, 1951, US)
Rainmaker, The (Francis Ford Coppola, 1997, US)
Raising Arizona (Joel Coen, 1987, US)
Raising Cain (Brian De Palma, 1992, US)
Rancid Aluminium (Edward Thomas, 2000, UK)
Rashômon (Akira Kurosawa, 1950, Japan)
Raw Deal (Anthony Mann, 1948, US)
Rear Window (Alfred Hitchcock, 1954, US)
Rebecca (Alfred Hitchcock, 1940, US)

Rebel Without a Cause (Nicholas Ray, 1955, US)
Red Dragon (Brett Ratner, 2002, US)
Red Eye (Wes Craven, 2005, US)
Red Rock West (John Dahl, 1992, US)
Regeneration (Raoul Walsh, 1915, US)
Renaissance (Christian Volckman, 2006, France/UK/Luxembourg)
Reservoir Dogs (Quentin Tarantino, 1992, US)
Reversal of Fortune (Barbet Schroeder, 1990, US)
Reversible Errors (Mike Robe, 2004, TV, US)
Ricochet (Russell Mulcahy, 1991, US)
Rififi chez les hommes, Du/Rififi (Jules Dassin, 1955, France)
Ripley's Game (Liliana Cavani, 2002, Italy/UK/USA)
Ripley Underground (Roger Spottiswoode, 2005, US/UK/Germany)
Rise and Fall of Legs Diamond, The (Budd Boetticher, 1960, US)
River's Edge (Tim Hunter, 1986, US)
Road to Perdition (Sam Mendes, 2002, US)
Roaring Twenties, The (Raoul Walsh, 1939, US)
Robbery (Peter Yates, 1967, UK)
Robocop (Paul Verhoeven, 1987, US)
Romeo is Bleeding (Peter Medak, 1993, UK/US)
Rookie, The (Clint Eastwood, 1990, US)
Rope (Alfred Hitchcock, 1948, US)
Runaway Jury (Gary Fleder, 2003, US)
Sabotage (Alfred Hitchcock, 1936, UK)
Saboteur (Alfred Hitchcock, 1942, US)
St Valentine's Day Massacre, The (Roger Corman, 1967, US)
Salamander, The (Peter Zinner, 1980, US/UK/Italy)
Samourai, Le/Samourai (Jean-Pierre Melville, 1967, France)
Scarface aka *Scarface, The Shame of the Nation* (Howard Hawks, 1932, US)
Scarface (Brian De Palma, 1983, US)
Scarlet Claw, The (Roy William Neill, 1944, US)
Scarlet Clue, The (Phil Rosen, 1945, US)
Scarlet Street (Fritz Lang, 1945, US)
Sea of Love (Harold Becker, 1989, US)
Secret Agent, The (Alfred Hitchcock, 1936, US)
Serpico (Sidney Lumet, 1973, US)
Set It Off (F. Gary Gray, 1996, US)
Set-Up, The (Robert Wise, 1949, US)
Se7en (David Fincher, 1995, US)
Seven-Ups, The (Philip D'Antoni, 1973, US)

Sexy Beast (Jonathan Glazer, 2000, UK/Spain)
Shadow of a Doubt (Alfred Hitchcock, 1943, US)
Shadow of the Thin Man (W. S. Van Dyke, 1941, US)
Shaft (Gordon Parks Jr, 1971, US)
Shaft (John Singleton, 2000, US)
Shaft's Big Score! (Gordon Parks, Jr, 1972, US)
Shaft in Africa (John Guillermin, 1973, US)
Shallow Grave (Danny Boyle, 1994, Scotland)
Shanghai Cobra, The (Phil Karlson, 1945, US)
Shattered (Wolfgang Petersen, 1991, US)
Shawshank Redemption, The (Frank Darabont, 1994, US)
Sheba Baby (William Girdler, 1975, US)
Sherlock Holmes (Albert Parker, 1922, US)
Sherlock Holmes (William K. Howard, 1932, US)
Sherlock Holmes and the Masks of Death aka *Masks of Death* (Roy Ward Baker,
    1984, UK)
Sherlock Holmes and the Secret Weapon (Roy William Neill, 1942, US)
Sherlock Holmes and the Spider Woman (Roy William Neill, 1944, US)
Sherlock Holmes and the Voice of Terror (John Rawlins, 1942, US)
Sherlock Holmes Baffled (Arthur Marrin, 1900, US)
Sherlock Holmes Faces Death (Roy William Neill, 1943, US)
Sherlock Holmes in Washington (Roy William Neill, 1943, US)
Sherlock, Jr (Buster Keaton, 1924, US)
Shining, The (Stanley Kubrick, 1980, US)
Shoot to Kill (Roger Spottiswoode, 1988, US)
Shopping (Paul Anderson, 1994, UK)
Sign of Four, The (Graham Cutts, 1932, UK)
Sign of Four, The (Desmond Davis, 1983, UK)
Silence of the Lambs, The (Jonathan Demme, 1991, US)
Sin City (Frank Miller, Robert Rodriguez and Quentin Tarantino, 2004, US)
Sin City 2 (Frank Miller and Robert Rodriguez, 2008, US)
Sin City 3 (Frank Miller and Robert Rodriguez, 2008, US)
Single White Female (Barbet Schroeder, 1992, US)
Sisters (Brian De Palma, 1973, US)
Sleeping Cardinal, The aka *Sherlock Holmes' Final Hour* (Leslie Hiscott, 1931, UK)
Sleeping With the Enemy (Joseph Ruben, 1991, US)
Sliver (Philip Noyce, 1993, US)
Small Time (Shane Meadows, 1996, UK)
Small Time Crooks (Woody Allen, 2000, US)
Small World of Sammy Lee, The (Ken Hughes, 1963, UK)

Snatch (Guy Ritchie, 2000, UK)
Song of the Thin Man, The (Edward Buzzell, 1947, US)
Sono otoko, kyôbô ni tsuki/Violent Cop (Takeshi Kitano, 1989, Japan)
Sorry, Wrong Number (Anatole Litvak, 1948, US)
South Central (Steve Anderson, 1992, US)
Speed (Jan de Bont, 1994, US)
Speed 2: Cruise Control (Jan de Bont, 1997, US)
Spellbound (Alfred Hitchcock, 1945, US)
Spider, The (Maurice Elvey, 1940, UK)
Spinnen, Die/Spiders (Fritz Lang, 1919, Germany)
Spione/Spies (Fritz Lang, 1928, Germany)
Spiral Staircase, The (Robert Siodmak, 1945, US)
Spivs (Colin Teague, 2003, UK)
Spoorloos/The Vanishing (George Sluizer, 1988, the Netherlands)
Squeeze, The (Michael Apted, 1977, UK)
Stage Fright (Alfred Hitchcock, 1950, US)
Star Chamber, The (Peter Hyams, 1983, US)
State of Grace (Phil Joanou, 1990, US)
Stepfather, The (Joseph Ruben, 1987, US)
Still of the Night (Robert Benton, 1982, US)
Sting, The (George Roy Hill, 1973, US)
Stormy Monday (Mike Figgis, 1988, UK)
Story of the Kelly Gang, The (Charles Tait, 1906, Australia)
Straight Out of Brooklyn (Matty Rice, 1991, US)
Strange Affair, The (David Greene, 1968, UK)
Strange Love of Martha Ivers, The (Lewis Milestone, 1946, US)
Stranger, The (Orson Welles, 1946, US)
Stranger Beside Me, The (Paul Shapiro, 2003, TV, US)
Stranger on the Third Floor, The (Boris Ingster, 1940, US)
Strangers on a Train (Alfred Hitchcock, 1951, US)
Strangler, The (Burt Topper, 1964, US)
Strasse, Die/The Street (Karl Grune, 1923, Germany)
Straw Dogs (Sam Peckinpah, 1971, UK/US)
Street With No Name, The (William Keighley, 1948, US)
Sudden Fear (David Miller, 1952, US)
Sudden Impact (Clint Eastwood, 1983, US)
Suddenly (Lewis Allen, 1954, US)
Sunset Boulevard (Billy Wilder, 1950, US)
Superfly (Gordon Parks Jr, 1972, US)
Suspect (Peter Yates, 1987, US)

Suspect Zero (E. Elias Merhige, 2004, US)

Suspicion (Alfred Hitchcock, 1941, US)

Suture (Scott McGehee and David Siegel, 1993, US)

S. W. A. T. (Clark Johnson, 2003, US)

Sweeney! (David Wickes, 1976, UK)

Sweeney 2 (Tom Clegg, 1978, UK)

Sweet Sweetback's Baadasssss Song (Melvin Van Peebles, 1971, US)

Swoon (Tom Kalin, 1992, US)

Tagebuch einer Verlorenen, Das/Diary of a Lost Girl (G. W. Pabst, 1929, Germany)

Taking of Pelham One Two Three, The (Joseph Sargent, 1974, US)

Talented Mr. Ripley, The (Anthony Minghella, 1999, US)

Tausend Augen des Dr Mabuse, Die/The Thousand Eyes of Dr Mabuse (Fritz Lang, 1960, West Germany)

Taxi Driver (Martin Scorsese, 1976, US)

Ten Little Indians (George Pollock, 1965, UK/US)

Ten Little Indians (Alan Birkinshaw, 1989, UK)

Ten Minutes to Live (Oscar Micheaux, 1932, US)

10 Rillington Place (Richard Fleischer, 1970, US/UK)

Ten to Midnight (J. Lee Thompson, 1983, US)

Terror, The (Richard Bird, 1938, UK)

Terror by Night (William Neill, 1946, US)

Testament des Dr Mabuse, Das/The Testament of Dr Mabuse (Fritz Lang, 1933, Germany)

They Call Me Mr Tibbs (Gordon Douglas, 1970, US)

They Live By Night (Nicholas Ray, 1948, US)

They Made Me a Criminal (Busby Berkeley, 1939, US)

They Made Me a Fugitive (Alberto Cavalcanti, 1947, UK)

They Won't Forget (Mervyn LeRoy, 1937, US)

Thief (Michael Mann, 1981, US)

Thieves' Highway (Jules Dassin, 1949, US)

Thieves Like Us (Robert Altman, 1974, US)

Thin Blue Line, The (Errol Morris, 1988, US)

Things to Do in Denver When You're Dead (Gary Fleder, 1995, US)

Think Fast Mr Moto (Norman Foster, 1937, US)

Thin Man, The (W. S. Van Dyke, 1934, US)

Thin Man Goes Home, The (Richard Thorpe, 1944, US)

Third Man, The (Carol Reed, 1949, UK)

39 Steps, The (Alfred Hitchcock, 1935, UK)

This Gun For Hire (Frank Tuttle, 1942, US)

Thomas Crown Affair, The (Norman Jewison, 1968, US)

Thunderbolt and Lightfoot (Michael Cimino, 1974, US)

Thunderheart (Michael Apted, 1992, US)

Tightrope (Richard Tuggle, 1984, US)

Tih Minh (Louis Feuillade, 1918, France)

Tirez sur le pianiste/Shoot the Piano Player (Francois Truffaut, 1960, France)

To Catch a Thief (Alfred Hitchcock, 1955, US)

To Die For (Gus Van Sant, 1995, US)

To Kill a Mockingbird (Robert Mulligan, 1962, US)

To Live and Die In L.A (William Friedkin, 1985, US)

Tony Rome (Gordon Douglas, 1967, US)

Topkapi (Jules Dassin, 1964, US)

Touchez pas au grisbi/Honour Among Thieves (Jacques Becker, 1954, France/
    Italy)

Touch of Evil (Orson Welles, 1958, US)

Tough Guys Don't Dance (Norman Mailer, 1987, US)

Traffic (Steven Soderbergh, 2000, US)

Traffic in Lost Souls (George Loane Tucker, 1913, US)

Traffik (Alistair Reid, 1989, TV, UK)

Training Day (Antoine Fuqua, 2001, US)

Tread Softly Stranger (Gordon Parry, 1958, UK)

Trial, The aka *Le Procès* (Orson Welles, 1962, France)

Trial by Jury (Heywood Gould, 1994, US)

Trial of Mary Dugan, The (Bayard Veiller, 1929, US)

Trois (Rob Hardy, 2000, US)

Trouble With Harry, The (Alfred Hitchcock, 1955, US)

True Romance (Tony Scott, 1993, US)

Twelve Angry Men (Sidney Lumet, 1957, US)

Two Jakes, The (Jack Nicholson, 1990, US)

Underneath, The (Steven Soderbergh, 1995, US)

Underworld (Oscar Micheaux, 1937, US)

Underworld aka *Paying the Penalty* (Josef Von Sternberg, 1927, US)

Underworld USA (Samuel Fuller, 1961, US)

Unfaithful (Adrian Lyne, 2002, US)

Unlawful Entry (Jonathan Kaplan, 1992, US)

Untouchables, The (Brian De Palma, 1987, US)

Usual Suspects, The (Bryan Singer, 1995, US)

U Turn (Oliver Stone, 1997, US)

Valachi Papers, The (Terence Young, 1972, US/Italy)

Vampires, Les/The Vampires (Louis Feuillade, 1915, France)

Vanishing, The (George Sluizer, 1993, US)

Verdict, The (Sidney Lumet, 1982, US)
Vertigo (Alfred Hitchcock, 1958, US)
Victim (Basil Dearden, 1961, UK)
Vierde man, De/The Fourth Man (Paul Verhoeven, 1983, Holland)
Villain (Michael Tuchner, 1971, UK)
V. I. Warshawski (Jeff Kanew, 1991, US)
Wachsfigurenkabinett, Das/Waxworks (Paul Leni, 1924, Germany)
Walking Tall (Phil Karlson, 1973, US)
Wall Street (Oliver Stone, 1987, US)
Weekend, Le/Weekend (Jean-Luc Godard, 1967, France)
What Ever Happened to Baby Jane? (Robert Aldrich, 1962, US)
What Lies Beneath (Robert Zemeckis, 2000, US)
When a Stranger Calls (Fred Walton, 1979, US)
When a Stranger Calls (Simon West, 2006, US)
Where The Sidewalk Ends (Otto Preminger, 1950, US)
While She Was Out (Susan Montford, 2008, US)
White Heat (Raoul Walsh, 1949, US)
White Mischief (Michael Radford, 1987, UK)
Wicker Man, The (Robin Hardy, 1973, UK)
Wicker Man, The (Neil LaBute, 2006, US)
Wide Boy (Ken Hughes, 1952, UK)
Wild At Heart (David Lynch, 1990, US)
Wild One, The (László Benedek,1953, US)
Wild Things (John McNaughton, 1998, US)
Witness (Peter Weir, 1985, US)
Witness for the Prosecution (Billy Wilder, 1957, US)
Who Framed Roger Rabbit? (Robert Zemeckis, 1988, US)
Woman in the Window, The (Fritz Lang, 1944, US)
Woman In White, The (1912, directors unknown, two silent versions, both US)
Woman Who Dared (Director unknown, 1911, Yankee serial, US)
Wrong Man, The (Alfred Hitchcock, 1957, US)
Yakuza, The (Sydney Pollack, 1974, US)
Year of the Dragon, The (Michael Cimino, 1985, US)
Yellow Claw, The (R. Plaisetty, 1920, UK)
Ying hung boon sik/A Better Tomorrow (John Woo, 1986, Hong Kong)
You Can't Get Away With It (Charles E. Ford, 1936, US)
Young Americans, The (Danny Cannon, 1993, UK)
You're Dead (Andy Hurst, 1998, UK)
Zodiac (David Fincher, 2007, US)

BIBLIOGRAPHY

Primary texts

Note: These are essential readings in the field of crime films, or provide useful overviews to crime cinema or to its many sub-types, including the police, gangster, film noir, mystery, erotic thriller and serial killer film.

Bould, M. (2005) *Film Noir: From Berlin to Sin City*. London and New York: Wallflower Press.

Chibnall, S. and R. Murphy (eds) (1999) *British Crime Cinema*. London: Routledge.

Hardy, P. (ed.) (1997) *BFI Companion to Crime*. Los Angeles: University of California Press.

_____ (1998) *The Overlook Film Encyclopedia: The Gangster Film*. Woodstock: Overlook Press.

Hirsch, F. (1999) *Detours and Lost Highways: A Map of Neo-Noir*. New York: Limelight.

_____ (2001) *The Dark Side of the Screen: Film Noir*. New York: A.S. Barnes.

Jenkins, P. (1994) *Using Murder: The Social Construction of Serial Homicide*. New York: De Gruyter.

Leitch, T. (2002) *Crime Films*. Cambridge: Cambridge University Press.

Morrison, K. (1999) 'The Technology of Homicide: Constructions of Evidence and Truth in the American Murder Film', in C. Sharrett (ed.) *Mythologies of Violence in Postmodern Media*. Detroit: Wayne State University Press, 301–18.

Munby, J. (1999) *Public Enemies, Public Heroes: Screening the Gangster from Little Caesar to Touch of Evil*. Chicago: University of Chicago Press.

Murphy, R. (1993) *Smash and Grab: Gangsters in the London Underworld 1920–1960*. London: Faber & Faber.

Naremore, J. (1998) *More Than Night: Film Noir in Its Contexts*. Berkeley: University of California Press.

Priestman, M. (2003) *The Cambridge Companion to Crime Fiction*. Cambridge: Cambridge University Press.

Prince, S. (ed.) (2000) *Screening Violence*. New Brunswick: Rutgers University Press.

_____ (2003) *Classical Film Violence: Designing and Regulating Brutality in Hollywood Cinema, 1930–1968*. New Brunswick: Rutgers University Press.

Pyrhönen, H. (1994) *Murder From an Academic Angle: An Introduction to the Study of the Detective Narrative*. Columbia, SC: Camden House.

Rafter, N. (2006) *Shots in the Mirror: Crime Films and Society*. Revised edition. New York: Oxford University Press.

Rubin, M. (1999) *Thrillers*. Cambridge: Cambridge University Press.

Simpson, P. L. (2000) *Psycho Paths: Tracking the Serial Killer Through Contemporary American Film and Fiction*. Carbondale: Southern Illinois University Press.

Slotkin, R. (2000 [1973]) *Regeneration Through Violence: The Mythology of the American Frontier*. Norman, OK: University of Oklahoma Press.

_____ (1992) *Gunfighter Nation: The Myth of the Frontier in Twentieth Century America*. New York: Atheneum.

Spicer, A. (2002) *Film Noir*. New York: Longman.

Williams, L. R. (2005) *The Erotic Thriller in Contemporary Cinema*. Bloomington: Indiana University Press.

Secondary texts

Additional, more specialised recommended reading.

Aguado, V. L. (2002) 'Film Genre and Its Vicissitudes: The Case of the Psychothriller', *Atlantis*, 24, 2 (June), 163–72.

Allen, R. and S. Ishii-Gonzales (eds) (1999) *Alfred Hitchcock: Centenary Essays*. London: British Film Institute.

Arroyo, J, (ed.) (2000) *Action/Spectacle Cinema*. London: British Film Institute.

Auden, W. H. (1938) 'The Guilty Vicarage', reprinted in R. W. Winks (ed.) (1980) *Detective Fiction: A Collection of Critical Essays*. Englewood Cliffs, NJ: Prentice-Hall, 15-24.

Barefoot, G. (2001) *Gaslight Melodrama: From Victorian London to 1940s Hollywood*. New York: Continuum.

Barnes, A. (2007) *Sherlock Holmes on Screen: The Complete Film and TV History*. 3rd revised edition. Richmond: Reynolds and Hearn.

Barnouw, Erik (1966–70) *The Image Empire, A History of Broadcasting in the United States*, 3 vols. New York: Oxford University Press.

_____ (1990) *Tube of Plenty: The Evolution of American Television*. Revised edition.

New York: Oxford University Press.

Barthes, R. (1975) *The Pleasure of the Text*, trans. R. Miller. New York: Noonday.

Barton, S. (2002) 'Your Self Storage: Female Investigation and Male Performativity in the Woman's Psychothriller', in G. Turner (ed.) *The Film Cultures Reader*. New York: Routledge, 187–216.

Bataille, G. (1985) *Visions of Excess: Selected Writings, 1927–1939*, trans. A. Stoekl with C. R. Lovitt and D. M. Leslie, Jr. Minneapolis: University of Minnesota Press.

_____ (1988) *The Accursed Share: An Essay on General Economy*, vol. 1, trans. R. Hurley. New York: Zone Books.

Berliner, T. (2001) 'The Genre Film as Booby Trap: 1970s Genre Bending and *The French Connection*', *Cinema Journal*, 40, 3, 25–46.

Berrettini, M. (1999) 'Private Knowledge, Public Space: Investigation and Navigation in *Devil in a Blue Dress*', *Cinema Journal*, 39, 1, 74–89.

Black, D. A. (1999) *Law in Film: Resonance and Representation*. Urbana: University of Illinois Press.

Black, J. (1991) *The Aesthetics of Murder: A Study in Romantic Literature and Contemporary Culture*. Baltimore: Johns Hopkins University Press.

Botting, F. (1995) *Gothic*. New York: Routledge.

Bowser, E. (1990) *The Transformation of the Cinema, 1907–1915: History of the American Cinema, vol. 2*. Berkeley: University of California Press.

Browne, N. (ed.) (2000) *Francis Ford Coppola's The Godfather Trilogy*. Cambridge: Cambridge University Press.

Browne, N. (2000) 'Fearful A-Symmetries: Violence as History in the Godfather Films (Introduction)', in N. Browne (ed) (2000) *Francis Ford Coppola's The Godfather Trilogy*. Cambridge: Cambridge University Press, 1–22.

Brunsdon, C. (1998) 'Structure of Anxiety: Recent British Television Crime Fiction', *Screen*, 39, 3, 223–43.

Buss, R. (1994) *French Film Noir*. New York: Marion Boyars.

Callahan, V. (2005) *Zones of Anxiety: Movement, Musidora, and the Crime Serials of Louis Feuillade*. Detroit: Wayne State University Press.

Cameron, I. (1975) *A Pictorial History of Crime Films*. New York: Hamlyn.

Carroll, N. (1990) *The Philosophy Of Horror; or Paradoxes of the Heart*. New York: Routledge.

Casillio, R. (2007) *Gangster Priest: The Italian-American Cinema of Martin Scorsese*. Toronto: University of Toronto Press.

Cawelti, J. (1976) *Adventure, Mystery and Romance: Formula Stories as Art and Popular Culture*. Chicago: University of Chicago Press.

Chandler, R. (1944) 'The Simple Art of Murder', *Atlantic Monthly*, December, 53–4.

Chesterton, G. K. (1946 [1902]) 'A Defence of Detective Stories', in H. Haycraft (ed.) *The Art of Mystery Stories*. New York: Dodd, Mead, 3–6.

Chibnall, S. (2001) 'Underworld England: Guy Ritchie and the British Gangster Film', *FilmHäftet*, 118, 6, 1–7.

Clarens, C. (1997) *Crime Movies: An Illustrated History of the Gangster Genre from D.W. Griffith to Pulp Fiction*. New York: Da Capo.

Clarke, A. (1992) '"You're Nicked!": Television Police Series and the Fictional Representation of Law and Order', in D. Strinati and S. Wagg (eds) *Come on Down? Popular Media Culture in Post-war Britain*. London: Verso, 232–53.

Clover, C. (1992) *Men, Women and Chainsaws: Gender in the Modern Horror Film*. Princeton: Princeton University Press.

_____ (2000) 'Judging Audiences; The Case of the Trial Movie', in C. Gledhill and L. Williams (eds) *Reinventing Film Studies*. London: Arnold, 244–64.

Cohan, S. (1998) 'Censorship and Narrative Indeterminacy in *Basic Instinct*', in S. Neale and M. Smith (eds) *Contemporary Hollywood Cinema*. New York: Routledge, 263–79.

Cole, S. A. (2001) *Suspect Identities: A History of Fingerprinting and Criminal Identification*. Cambridge: Harvard University Press.

Cooke, L. (2001) 'The Police Series', in G. Creeber (ed.) *The Television Genre Book*. London: British Film Institute.

Copjec, J. (ed.) (1993) *Shades of Noir: A Reader*. London: Verso.

Daly, M. and M. Wilson (eds) (1988) *Homicide*. New York: De Gruyter.

Dawson, G. (2000) *Quentin Tarantino: The Cinema of Cool*. New York: Applause.

Denvir, J. (ed.) (1996) *Legal Reelism: Movies as Legal Texts*. Austin: University of Texas Press.

Dimenberg, E. (2004) *Film Noir and the Spaces of Modernity*. Cambridge: Harvard University Press.

Doane, M. A. (1991) *Femmes Fatales: Feminism, Film Theory, Psychoanalysis*. New York: Routledge.

Douglas, J. and M. Olshaker (1997) *Journey Into Darkness*. New York: Scribner.

Doyle. A. (2003) *Arresting Images: Crime and Policing In Front of the Television Camera*. Toronto: University of Toronto Press.

Dyer, R. (1999) *Seven*. London: British Film Institute.

Egger, S. (1990) *Serial Murder: An Elusive Phenomenon*. New York: Praegar.

Everson, W. (1972) *The Detective in Film*. Secaucus, N.J. : Citadel Press.

Feasey, R. (2003) 'Sex, Controversy, Box-Office: From Blockbuster to Bonkbuster', in J. Stringer (ed.) *Movie Blockbusters*. Routledge: New York, 167–77.

Foucault, M. (ed.) (1975) *I Pierre Rivière, Having Slaughtered my Mother, my Sister and my Brother ... a Case of Parricide in the Nineteenth Century*. Lincoln: University Of Nebraska Press.

_____ (1995 [1977]) *Discipline and Punish: The Birth of the Prison*. New York: Vintage.

Friedman, L. M. (1993) *Crime and Punishment in American History*. New York: HarperCollins.

Gabbard, K. and G. O. Gabbard (1987) *Psychiatry and the Cinema*. Chicago: University of Chicago Press.

Gardaphe, F. (2006) *From Wiseguys to Wise Men: The Gangster and Italian American Masculinities*. New York: Routledge

Geberth, V. J. (2006) *Practical Homicide Investigation: Tactics, Procedures and Forensic Techniques*. 4th edition. Boca Raton: CRC Press.

Gifford, D. (1986) *The British Film Catalogue 1895–1985*. London: David & Charles.

Gilman, S. L. (1985) *Difference and Pathology: Stereotypes of Sexuality, Race and Madness*. Ithaca: Cornell University Press.

Girard, R. (1979) *Violence and the Sacred*, trans. P. Gregory. Baltimore: Johns Hopkins University Press.

_____ (1986) *The Scapegoat*. Baltimore: Johns Hopkins University Press.

Glamuzina, J. and A. Laurie (1991) *Parker and Hulme: A Lesbian View*. Auckland: New Women's Press.

Gledhill, C. (1998 [1978]) '*Klute* 1: a Contemporary Film Noir and Feminist Film Criticism', in E. Ann Kaplan (ed.) *Women in Film Noir*. London: BFI, 20–34.

_____ (1998 [1978]) '*Klute* 2: Feminism and *Klute*', in E. Ann Kaplan (ed.) *Women in Film Noir*. London: BFI, 99–114.

Glynn, K. (2000) *Tabloid Culture: Trash Taste, Popular Power and the Transformation of American Television*. Durham: Duke University Press.

Goodwin, S.W. & E. Bronfen (2006) *Death and Representation*. Baltimore: John Hopkins University Press.

Grant, B. K. (ed.) (1996) *The Dread of Difference: Gender and the Horror Film*. Austin: University of Texas Press.

_____ (1998) 'Rich and Strange: The Yuppie Horror Film', in S. Neale and M. Smith (eds) *Contemporary Hollywood Cinema*. New York: Routledge, 280–93.

Gunning, T. (1995) 'Tracing the Individual Body: Photography, Detectives and Early Cinema', in L. Charney and V. R. Schwartz (eds) *Cinema and the Invention of Modern Life*. Berkeley: University of California Press, 15–45.

Haeffner, N. (2005) *Alfred Hitchcock*. Pearson Longman: London.

Haining, P. (1994) *The Television Sherlock Holmes*. New York: Carol Publishing.

Halttunen, K. (1998) *Murder Most Foul: The Killer and the American Gothic Imagination*. Cambridge, MA: Harvard University Press.

Hart, L. (1994) *Fatal Women: Lesbian Sexuality and the Mark of Aggression*. Princeton: Princeton University Press.

Haydock, R. (1978) *Deerstalker!: Holmes and Watson On Screen*. Metuchen: Scarecrow.

Hunt, L. (1999) 'Dog Eat Dog: The Squeeze and the *Sweeney* Films', in S. Chibnall and R. Murphy (eds) *British Crime Cinema*. London: Routledge, 134–47.

Inciardi, J. A. and J. L. Dee (1987) 'From the Keystone Cops to *Miami Vice*: Images of Policing in American Popular Culture', *Journal of Popular Culture*, 21, 2, 84–102.

Jameson, F. (1983 [1970]) 'On Raymond Chandler', reprinted in G. W. Most and W. W. Stowe (eds) *Poetics of Murder*. New York: Harcourt Brace Jovanovich, 122–48.

Jarvis, R. M. and P. R. Joseph (eds) (1998) *Prime Time Law: Fictional Television as Legal Narrative*. Durham: Carolina Academic Press.

Jermyn, D. (2006) Crime Watching: Investigating Real Crime TV. London: I.B. Tauris.

Kamir, O. (2006) *Framed: Women in Law and Film*. Durham: Duke University Press.

Kaplan, E. A. (ed.) (1990) *Psychoanalysis and the Cinema*. New York: Routledge.

_____ (ed.) (1998 [1978]) *Women in Film Noir*. Revised edition. London: British Film Institute.

Kerr, P. (1979/80) 'Out of What Past? Notes on the "B" Film Noir', *Screen Education*, 32, 33, Autumn/Winter, 45–65, reprinted in A. Silver & J. Ursini. (eds) (1996) *Film Noir Reader*. New York: Limelight, 107–27.

Krutnik, F. (1991) *In a Lonely Street: Film Noir, Genre, Masculinity*. New York: Routledge.

Lay, S. (2002) *British Social Realism: From Documentary to Brit Grit*. London and New York: Wallflower Press.

Lebeau, V. (2001) *Psychoanalysis and Cinema: The Play of Shadows*. London and New York: Wallflower Press.

Lee, S. (2003) 'These Are Our Stories: Trauma, Form and the Screen Phenomenon of *Law and Order*', *Discourse*, 25, 1/2, 81–97.

Lesser, W. (1993) *Pictures at an Execution: An Enquiry into the Subject of Murder*. Cambridge: Harvard University Press.

Lichtenfeld, E. (2004) *Action Speaks Louder: Violence, Spectacle and the American Action Movie*. Revised edition. Westport, CT: Praeger.

Lucia, C. (2005) *Framing Female Lawyers: Women on Trial In Film*. Austin: University of Texas Press.

Maloney, J. J. (1998) 'The Crime Film', *Crime Magazine: An Encyclopedia of Crime*. On-line. Available http://crimemagazine.com/crimefilm.htm (accessed 4 December 2005).

Man, G. (2000) 'Ideology and Genre in the *Godfather* Films' in N. Browne (ed.) *Francis Ford Coppola's The Godfather Trilogy*. Cambridge: Cambridge University Press, 109–32.

Massood, P. (2003) *Black City Cinema: African-American Urban Experiences in Film*. Philadelphia: Temple University Press.

McArthur, C. (1972) *Underworld USA*. London: Warburg.

McKenna, A. J. (1996) 'Pubic Execution', in J. Denvir (ed.) *Legal Reelism: Movies as Legal Texts*. Urbana: University of Illinois Press, 225–43.

Mitchell, E. (1986) 'Apes and Essences: Some Sources of Significance in the American Gangster Film', in B. K. Grant (ed.) *Film Genre Reader*. Austin: University of Texas, 159–68.

Mizejewski, L. (2004) *Hard Boiled and High Heeled: The Woman Detective in Popular Culture*. New York: Routledge.

Modleski, T. (1989) *The Women Who Knew Too Much: Hitchcock and Feminist Theory*. Revised edition. New York: Routledge.

Morrison, T. and C. Brodsky Lacour (eds) (1997) *Birth of a Nationhood: Gaze, Script and Spectacle in the OJ Simpson Case*. New York: Pantheon.

Most, G. W. and W. W. Stowe (eds) (1983) *The Poetics of Murder: Detective Fiction and Literary Theory*. New York: Harcourt Brace Jovanovich.

Mulvey, L. (1999 [1975]) 'Visual Pleasure and Narrative Cinema', in R. Stam and T. Miller (eds) *Film and Theory: An Anthology*. New York: Blackwell, 483–509.

Nicholls, M. (2004) *Scorsese's Men: Melancholia and the Mob*. Melbourne, Australia: Pluto Press.

Page, F. (2005) *Quintessential Tarantino: The Films of Quentin Tarantino*. London: Marion Boyars.

Peary, G. (2007) *Quentin Tarantino: Interviews*. Jackson: University of Mississippi Press.

Pelizzon V. P. and N. M. West (2001) 'Good Stories from the Mean Streets: Weegee and Hard-Boiled Autobiography', *The Yale Journal of Criticism*, 17, 1, 20–50.

Phillips, S., M. Haworth-Booth and C. Squiers (1997) *Police Pictures: The Photograph as Evidence*. San Francisco: Chronicle.

Pidduck, J. (1995) 'The 1990s Hollywood Fatal Femme: (Dis)Figuring Feminism, Family, Irony, Violence', *Cinéaction* 38, 64–72.

Pinedo, I. C. (1997) *Recreational Terror: Women and the Pleasures of Horror Film Viewing*. Albany: SUNY Press.

Pomerance, M. and J. Sakeris (eds) (2000) *Bang Bang, Shoot Shoot! Essays on Guns and Popular Culture*. 2nd edition. New York: Pearson.

Porfirio, R., A. Silver, and J. Ursini. (2002) *Film Noir Reader 3*. New York: Limelight.

Potter, C. Bond (1998) *War on Crime: Bandits, G-Men and the Politics of Mass Culture*. New Brunswick: Rutgers University Press.

Rabinowitz, P. (2002) *Black and White and Noir: America's Pulp Modernism*. New York: Columbia University Press.

Raczkowski, C. (2003) 'From Modernity's Detection to Modernist Detectives: Narrative Vision in the Work of Allan Pinkerton and Dashiell Hammett', *Modern Fiction Studies*, 49, 4, 629–59.

Ramsland, K. (2001) *The Forensic Science of CSI*. New York: Berkeley Boulevard.

Rapping, E. (2003) *Law and Justice as Seen on TV*. New York: New York University Press.

Reiner, R. (2002) 'Media Made Criminality: The Representation of Crime in the Mass Media', in R. Reiner, M. Maguire and R. Morgan (eds) *The Oxford Handbook of Criminology*. 3rd edition. Oxford: Oxford University Press, 376–416.

Ressler, R. and T. Shachtman (1992) *Whoever Fights Monsters*. New York: St Martin's Press.

Revitch, E. and L. B. Schlesinger (1981) *Psychopathology of Homicide*. Illinois: Charles Thomas.

Robertson, P. (2001) *Film Facts*. New York: Billboard.

Rohmer, E. and C. Chabrol (1979) *Hitchcock: The First Forty-Four Films*. New York: Ungar.

Rosenberg, N. (1994) 'Hollywood on Trials: Courts and Films, 1930–1960', *Law and History Review*, 12, 341–67.

_____ (1996) 'Law Noir', in J. Denvir (ed.) *Legal Reelism: Movies as Legal Texts*. Urbana: University of Illinois Press, 280–302.

Ruth, D. L. (1996) *Inventing the Public Enemy: The Gangster in American Culture, 1918–1934*. Chicago: University of Chicago Press.

Sayers, D. (1929) 'The Omnibus of Crime', reprinted in R. W. Winks (ed.) (1980) *Detective Fiction: A Collection of Critical Essays*. Englewood Cliffs, NJ: Prentice-Hall, 53–83.

_____ (1946) 'Aristotle on Detective Fiction', in R. W. Winks (ed.) (1980) *Detective Fiction: A Collection of Critical Essays*. Englewood Cliffs, NJ: Prentice-Hall, 25–34.

Schatz, T. (1981) *Hollywood Genres: Formulas, Filmmaking, and the Studio System*. Philadelphia: Temple University Press.

Sconce, J. (1993) 'Spectacles of Death: Identification, Reflexivity and Contemporary Horror' in J. Collins, H. Radner and A. Preacher Collins (eds) *Film Theory Goes to The Movies*. New York: Routledge, 103–119.

Seltzer, M. (1998) *Serial Killers: Death and Life in America's Wound Culture*. New York: Routledge.

Shadoian, J. (2002) *Dreams and Dead Ends*. Revised edition. Oxford: Oxford University Press.

Sharrett, C. (ed.) (1999) *Mythologies of Violence in Postmodern Media*. Detroit:

Wayne State University Press.

Sharrett, C. (1999) 'Introduction', in C. Sharrett (ed) (1999) *Mythologies of Violence in Postmodern Media*. Detroit: Wayne State University Press, 9–20.

_____ (1999) 'Afterword: Sacrificial Violence and Postmodern Ideology', in C. Sharrett (ed) (1999) *Mythologies of Violence in Postmodern Media*. Detroit: Wayne State University Press, 413–34.

Sheen, E and A. Davison (eds) (2004) *The Cinema of David Lynch: American Dreams, Nightmare Visions*. London and New York: Wallflower Press.

Silver, A. and E. Ward (eds) (1992) *Film Noir: An Encyclopedic Reference to the American Style*. 3rd edition. Woodstock: Overlook.

Silver, A. and J. Ursini (eds) (1996) *Film Noir Reader*. New York: Limelight.

_____ (eds) (1999) *Film Noir Reader 2*. New York: Limelight.

_____ (eds) (2004) *Film Noir Reader 4: The Crucial Films and Themes*. New York: Limelight.

_____ (eds) (2007) *The Gangster Film Reader*. New York: Limelight.

Sklar, R. (1992) *City Boys: Cagney, Bogart, Garfield*. Princeton: Princeton University Press.

_____ (2002) *Film: An International History of the Medium*. 2nd edition. New York: Prentice-Hall.

Slocum, J. D. (ed.) (2001) *Violence and American Cinema*. New York: Routledge.

Stasio, M. (2005) 'Make Way for TV's New Miss Marple, One With Some Romance in Her Past', *New York Times*, 15 April, B21.

Tatar, M. (1995) *Lustmord: Sexual Murder in Weimar Germany*. Princeton: Princeton University Press.

Thomas, R. R. (1994) 'The Dream of the Empty Camera: Image, Evidence and Authentic American Style in American Photographs and *Farewell My Lovely*', *Criticism*, 36, 415–57.

Tithecott, R. (1997) *Of Men and Monsters: Jeffrey Dahmer and the Construction of the Serial Killer*. Madison: University of Wisconsin Press.

Todorov, T. (1977) 'The Typology of Detective Fiction', in *The Poetics of Prose*, trans. R. Howard. Ithaca: Cornell University Press, 42–52.

Warshow, R. (2002 [1975]) 'The Gangster as Tragic Hero', in *The Immediate Experience: Movies, Comics, Theater and other Aspects of Popular Culture*. Revised edition. New York: Doubleday, 127–33.

Williams, L. R. (1993) 'Sisters Under the Skin: Video and Blockbuster Erotic Thrillers', in P. Cook and P. Dodd (eds) *Women and Film: A Sight and Sound Reader*. Philadelphia: Temple University Press, 105–14.

Wilson, R. W. (2003) 'Crime and the Mafia', in P. C. Rollins (ed.) *The Columbia Companion To American History*. New York: Columbia University Press, 509–17.

Wilt, D. E. (2003) 'Hollywood's Detective', in P. C. Rollins (ed.) *The Columbia Companion to American History*. New York: Columbia University Press, 583–89.

Winks, R. (ed.) (1980) *Detective Fiction: A Collection of Critical Essays*. 2nd edition. Englewood Cliffs, NJ: Prentice-Hall.

Yaquinto, M. (1998) *Pump 'Em Full of Lead: A Look at Gangsters on Film*. New York: Twayne.

INDEX